Taunton's COMPLETE ILLUSTRATED *Guide to*

Tablesaws

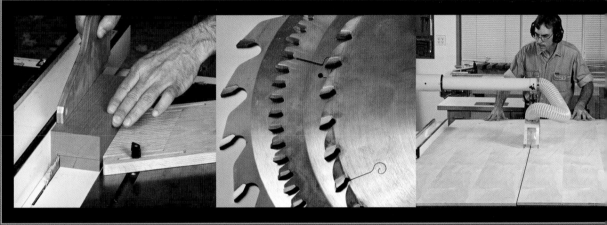

PAUL ANTHONY

The Taunton Press

The Taunton Press
Inspiration for hands-on living®

The Taunton Press, Inc., 63 South Main Street, P.O. Box 5506, Newtown, CT 06470-5506
e-mail: tp@taunton.com

EDITOR: Ken Burton
COPY EDITOR: Candace B. Levy
INDEXER: Cathy Goddard
JACKET/COVER DESIGN: Lori Wendin
INTERIOR DESIGN: Lori Wendin
LAYOUT: Cathy Cassidy
ILLUSTRATOR: Mario Ferro
PHOTOGRAPHER: Paul Anthony (except where noted)

LIBRARY OF CONGRESS CATALOGING-IN-PUBLICATION DATA
ANTHONY, PAUL, 1954-
   TAUNTON'S COMPLETE ILLUSTRATED GUIDE TO TABLESAWS / PAUL ANTHONY.
      P. CM.
   ISBN 978-1-60085-011-0
   1. CIRCULAR SAWS. 2. WOODWORKING TOOLS. I. TITLE. II. TITLE: COMPLETE ILLUSTRATED GUIDE TO TABLESAWS.
   TT186.A58 2009
   684'.083--DC22

                  2008032023

Printed in the United States of America
10 9 8 7 6 5 4 3 2 1

The following manufacturers/names appearing in *Taunton's Complete Illustrated Guide to Tablesaws* are trademarks: Accu-Miter®, Biesemeyer®, Biesemeyer's® snap-in spreader, Board Buddies®, Boeshield T-9®, Corian®, Craftsman®, Delta® Deluxe, Delta® Unisaw®, DeWALT®, Excalibur®, Excalibur's® Merlin® splitter, Ferrari®, Freud®, Freud's® Dial-A-Width Dado Set, General®, Grip-Tite®, GRR-Ripper®, Harbor Freight®, HTC® Products, Inc., Jet®, Laguna®, Laguna® TSS tablesaw, Lee Valley Tools®, LRH Enterprises®, LRH Enterprises® Magic Molder, Melamine®, Powermatic®, Ridgid®, Robland®, Saw Stop® tablesaw, Sears®, Simple Green®, Steel City® Toolworks, Unifence®, Wilsonart®, Woodcraft®, Woodhaven®, WD-40®

Working wood is inherently dangerous. Using hand or power tools improperly or ignoring safety practices can lead to permanent injury or even death. Don't try to perform operations you learn about here (or elsewhere) unless you're certain they are safe for you. If something about an operation doesn't feel right, don't do it. Look for another way. We want you to enjoy the craft, so please keep safety foremost in your mind whenever you're in the shop.

To Jerry and Linda,
for kick-starting my woodworking career so long ago.

Acknowledgments

As you might imagine, I had quite a bit of help with this book. Many thanks are due to the following good folks:

First of all, a tip o' the woodworker's cap to my pals Craig Bentzley, Walt Segl, Tony O'Malley, Steve Metz, Ken Burton, and Bil Mitchell, who opened their shops to me for photos of equipment and techniques. Special thanks to Craig, a real helper and adviser who also played "Mr. Hands" for many of the Section 10 photos. Speaking of photos, I'm indebted to my friend and videographer Benoit Bissonnette for processing and providing the video stills for the "Kickback in Action" photos on pp. 82–83.

Thanks to the following for providing tools for purposes of photography: Norm Frampton at General International, Norm Hubert at LRH Enterprises, Scott Box at Steel City Toolworks, Brad Witt at Woodhaven, Henry Wang at Micro Jig Inc., and Jerry Jaksha at Mesa Vista Design. My friends John Schaeffer and the crew at the Allentown, Pennsylvania, Woodcraft store were also gracious in allowing me to take photos in the classroom there.

On the editorial side, Helen Albert at The Taunton Press deserves credit for instigating this project and kudos for her patience into the eleventh hour. And this book would not be what it is without the incisive input and contributions from my editor, Ken Burton, a savvy woodworker and writer who understands the subject. Also in the realm of publishing, it wouldn't do to overlook my friend Kelly Mehler's tireless work in print and behind the scenes to make tablesaws safer machines to work with. My fingers salute you, Kelly!

Finally, and closest to home, eternal gratitude to my sweet Jean for her unflagging patience during the months and months of writing of this book. Whew!

Contents

Introduction

WHEN I BEGAN my woodworking career several decades ago, information on the craft was pretty scant. There were few available books on the subject and no woodworking magazines to speak of (if you can imagine that!). Like many other budding woodworkers of the day, I floundered through my self-education, making every mistake imaginable and then some.

Getting my first tablesaw was both exhilarating and daunting. On the one hand, I knew it was my ticket into the world of serious woodworking. On the other hand, well, I wasn't quite sure what to do with it. And you can bet that the sharp spinning blade made me just a bit nervous.

I remember wishing that the saw came with a truly useful owner's manual. I wanted something with lots of pictures and sensible instruction on ripping, crosscutting, joint making, and shaping—along with plans for cool, useful jigs. I craved information on blades, cutters, and safety. I wanted a shop-shelf reference that I could consult as my woodworking chops improved over time.

What I needed was the book you hold in your hands.

These pages are packed with sound, no-nonsense advice for both beginners and experienced tablesaw users. Whether you're searching for a new saw, trying to learn new techniques, puzzling over blade choices, or wondering how to make your saw perform better, you'll find the answers here, along with safety advice and plans for essential jigs. Consider this book a life-long friend and adviser at the tablesaw. May it help you enjoy your woodworking adventures throughout the years!

Best of luck. Stay safe and stay sharp.

—Paul Anthony

Choosing a Tablesaw

THE 10-IN. TABLESAW is the mainstay of many a woodshop. It's called a 10-in. saw because it spins a 10-in.-dia. blade. There are bigger saws (and a few smaller ones), but the 10-in. saw is the most common and is likely to be the saw most woodworkers start out with.

If you're reading this book, it's a good bet that either you own one of these tablesaws or you want one. And even if you already own one, it's the rare woodworker who doesn't think about upgrading. You've prob-ably noticed that there is a virtual fleet of models for sale, ranging from compact saws costing only $100 or so to large, industrial behemoths that might set you back many thousands of dollars.

In this section, I'll walk you through the available choices and try to note the advan-tages and disadvantages of each. I'll also point out the various features common to most tablesaws and provide some guidance as to what to look for as you compare saws from different manufacturers. Some of the

Tablesaws range from the mini to the mighty. The portable saw at left is great for job-site work, whereas profes-sional shops have long depended on cabinet saws like the Laguna model at right, equipped with a sliding table.

saw designs are proven standbys that have served the woodworking community for years. Others are new models that include welcome refinements and safety features unavailable until recently. Regardless of whether you're a hobbyist or a pro, there's a saw out there that will help you become a better woodworker.

Types of Saws

Just a few short decades ago, woodworkers had essentially two choices as to what tablesaw model to buy: a contractor's saw or a cabinet saw. The open-base contractor's saws were designed to be portable enough for jobsite work, while their heavier cabinet saw brothers were fixtures in both factories and smaller woodshops. The surge of small-shop woodworking that began in the early 1970s has led inexorably toward the development of a wealth of models designed to suit everyone from the budget-stretched beginner to the seasoned pro who cranks out dozens of projects a year.

These models include portable saws, contractor's saws, hybrid saws, cabinet saws, European-style saws, panel saws, and combination machines; all with their own pluses and minuses. What follows is a rundown of the field, which should give you an idea of what's available. As you consider your options, you'll want to base your choice on a number of factors, including the size of your shop space, the type and quality of work you do, your future woodworking aspirations, and of course your budget. One thought in regard to this last factor—a tablesaw is so critical to accurate, efficient woodworking, it is well worth buying the best you possibly can. Scrimp on some of your other tools if

you must, but I guarantee you won't be disappointed if you buy somewhat more tablesaw than you think you need.

Portable Saws

Portable tablesaws have come a long way in the last couple of decades. These small, lightweight units were primarily designed for carpenters because they can be easily transported to a job site. With its tough plastic body and aluminum top, a portable tablesaw typically weighs in at well under 100 lb. but can still take on carpentry chores like ripping 2×4s and plywood. Many manufacturers offer nicely designed, collapsible wheeled stands for easy mobility of their portable saws.

▶ CUTTING THROUGH THE TYPE HYPE

These days, it's getting harder and harder to categorize "types" of tablesaws because there is so much overlap in features. For example, contractor's saws have long been distinguished by their relative portability, open bases, and attachment of the motor carriage to the underside of the tabletop rather than to the cabinet. Now portable saws have superseded contractor's saws on the job site, while newer hybrid saws have enclosed bases and motor carriages that sometimes attach to the saw cabinet like cabinet saws. And although a panel saw is always a sliding tablesaw, the reverse isn't necessarily true. So don't feel alone if you're confused by marketing terms. When shopping for a saw, pay more attention to individual features than to the type of saw.

As an option, some manufacturers offer mobile collapsible stands for their portable saws.

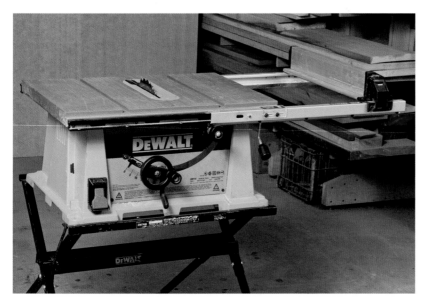

The rip capacity on this popular job-site saw is limited to about 25 in. On the plus side, the telescoping fence rails retract completely for easy storage.

Attractive to woodworkers who are pressed for shop space, portable saws can be easily stowed away under a bench when not in use. At $100 to $700 or so, they are relatively inexpensive compared to full-size saws. Of course, you get what you pay for. Portable models are less powerful, less durable, and generally less accurate. The rip capacity is also generally less than the larger models.

A portable saw may be a good choice if you focus mainly on basic home-improvement projects—utility shelving and the like. You'll be able to build cabinets and even simple furniture with it if you're willing to work within the saw's limitations. But if you have grander woodworking aspirations, you're likely to grow frustrated with a portable saw's small size and lack of power. It will struggle to rip thick hardwoods, and large sheet goods may teeter on the small top. Ripping capacity will also be somewhat limited due to the short fence rails.

These saws are generally driven by a universal, direct drive motor—the same kind you'll find on a router. The sawblade typically mounts directly on the motor arbor rather than to a separate belt-driven arbor. Count on doing some tweaking right out of the box to make the saw work well.

If you're a beginning woodworker on a tight budget, a decent portable saw might be your entry ticket to the world of woodworking. Just keep in mind that the better you become, the more frustrated you're likely to get with a portable saw—particularly an inexpensive model. You'll learn quickly why serious woodworkers trade up from a portable model to a better version.

[TIP] If you're serious at all about woodworking, steer away from the cheapest portable saws. You're already buying in at the low end. Don't overdo it.

Contractor's Saws

Originally designed for job-site use, the full-size, economically priced contractor's saws quickly found a home in many small workshops. With a footprint and table size

The "direct-drive" blade on a portable saw is mounted on the motor arbor, as seen on the upended saw at left. The internal mechanisms, such as the motor carriage trunnion at right, are lightweight compared to full-size saws.

comparable to a cabinet saw, a contractor's saw can handle the same work, just not quite as effectively.

A contractor's saw is easily recognized by its open base and chunky induction motor (typically $1^1/_2$ hp) that hangs off the rear of the saw. The dual-voltage motor, which drives the saw arbor via a single belt, can be wired for either 115v or 230v. You can either run it from standard household current or convert it to run more efficiently on 230v if your shop is wired for it. The short, open-backed sheet-metal base sits atop an open-frame stand. Another distinguishing characteristic of a contractor's saw is that the motor is attached with carriage bolts to the underside of the table.

A well-tuned contractor's saw outfitted with a good blade will perform all of the woodworking chores that a beefier cabinet saw will, at considerably less cost. The trade-off is primarily in power and overall heft. The table wings on a contractor's saw are typically stamped steel or cast web work, and the handwheels and other external fit-

The motor on a contractor's saw hangs from a plate off the rear of the saw. You can easily remove it when you need to transport the saw.

The motor carriage trunnions on contractor's saws are bolted to the underside of the table. All of the internal mechanisms are lighter duty than those on cabinet saws.

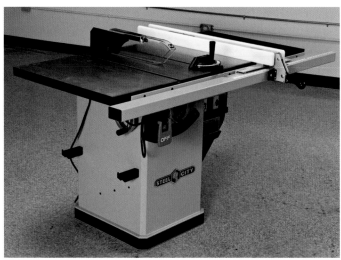

A hybrid saw blends features from contractor's saws and cabinet saws to provide an economical but competent alternative to a hardier cabinet saw.

tings are less substantial than on a cabinet saw. The motor carriage and other internal components are also lighter and leaner, and the power transfer of a single belt drive can't compare to the traction conveyed by the multiple belts on a cabinet saw. Ripping thick hardwoods can bog down a contractor's saw if the stock isn't fed slowly. However, it should handle softwoods, 3/4-in. hardwood, and most sheet goods with no problem.

Contractor's saws suffer from two thorny problems. The first is that the cantilevered motor causes the motor carriage to twist when the blade is tilted. This can lead to burning and increase the danger of kickback when making bevel cuts. The other problem is that the open base thwarts effective dust collection.

At prices ranging from about $500 to $900, a contractor's saw is a good entry-level tablesaw for the serious woodworker. You can often find great deals on used contractor's saws, which will work well if tuned up

properly. Because the motor can be easily removed to reduce weight, these saws are also a good choice for the small-shop woodworker who needs to bring a tablesaw on site occasionally. *Note:* Some industry experts speculate that contractor's saws will largely be supplanted by hybrid saws in the next few years.

Hybrid Saws

"Hybrid" tablesaws are a fairly recent addition to the marketplace. Designed as an economical cross between contractor's saws and cabinet saws, hybrids offer an enclosed cabinet. This eliminates the twisting of the motor carriage caused by a cantilevered motor like that on a contractor's saw. The enclosed cabinet also improves dust collection, especially if the saw includes a dust shroud around the blade.

The $1^3/4$-hp to 2-hp induction motor on a hybrid saw provides a bit more power than the one on a contractor's saw, but still can't

On some hybrid saws, the motor trunnions attach to the cabinet rather than to the underside of the table.

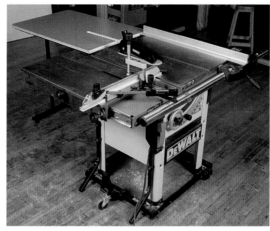

This hybrid saw from DeWALT® features an optional sliding table to make crosscutting chores a breeze.

match the strength of a standard cabinet saw. You can run a hybrid saw from 115v household current, while the minimum 3-hp motor on a cabinet saw requires 230v. The motor carriage and other internal mechanisms on hybrid saws are not as heavy duty as those on standard cabinet saws. On most hybrids, the trunnions attach to the underside of the table, but some manufacturers attach them to the cabinet instead. This makes aligning the table slots to the blade easier.

▶ See "Align the Blade and Miter Gauge Slot" on p. 105.

▶ TABLESAW TOOL TESTS

When shopping for particular saw models, you'll find woodworking magazines to be a great help. They often feature head-to-head tests of various saws on the market, comparing features, accuracy, power, fences, dust collection, and the like. Most magazines provide an online index that will steer you toward available back issues that contain tests on the various types of saws. Get the most current issue available, as new models appear regularly. You can also find tool reviews online. Just type the appropriate terms into a search engine (for example, "review of Laguna TSS tablesaw").

Overall, hybrid saws are an improvement over contractor's saws. As part of the package, you can expect a hybrid to come with a well-designed, accurate fence. Some models even offer an optional sliding table. At prices ranging from about $700 to $1,100, a hybrid saw might be a good bet for a woodworker who is looking for an economical alternative to a cabinet saw without the poor dust collection and bevel-ripping shortcomings of a contractor's saw.

The author's 10-in., 3-hp. Delta® Unisaw® is representative of many cabinet saws used for years in factories and commercial shops in the United States.

The trunnions, yoke, and sector gears in a cabinet saw are made from strong, heavy castings to resist twisting and vibration.

Cabinet Saws

Cabinet saws have long been the gold standard in U.S. shops. Named for its enclosed base, a cabinet saw is rock solid, heavy, and strong enough to plow through any kind of wood. Available in 10-in., 12-in., and larger models, a cabinet saw is equipped with a 3-hp or 5-hp induction motor (Some larger models have even more powerful motors.) In my experience, 3-hp is plenty for a 10-in. saw. I've never heard of a 3-hp motor stalling or overheating from stress, even during heavy use. Two or three belts ensure hearty power transmission from the motor to the arbor pulleys. The motor carriage trunnions attach to the cabinet, making for easy alignment of the table.

The enclosed base helps dust containment. Most saws have a dust-collection port in the base or can be fitted with one to suck out the swirling cloud of dust inside. However, unless the saw includes a dust shroud around the blade, don't be surprised to find piles of sawdust and chips at the bottom of the cabinet.

These machines are built to perform well and to last. The internal mechanisms are beefy and resistant to twisting and vibration that can compromise cuts. The overall rigidity of the motor carriage assembly ensures that stops and other adjustments will hold true. The cast-iron table and wings are also heavy, helping to dampen any vibration in use. Handwheels are usually large enough for easy operation, and external knobs and locking devices are sturdy and durable. These days, cabinet saws all come equipped with a premium fence that ensures accurate work. And most old models are easy enough to retrofit with a premium aftermarket fence.

All of these factors add up a machine that's strong, accurate, reliable, and satisfying to work with. If you're currently working with a contractor's saw or hybrid saw that seems underpowered for the type of work you're doing, it may be time to step up to a cabinet saw. At prices ranging from approximately $1,000 to $2,200, it's an investment for sure, but one that's certain to pay off in spades for serious woodworkers.

This European tablesaw includes a relatively narrow sliding table with an extended outrigger panel to help carry the workpiece.

European Saws

In the 1990s, European tablesaws started to make major inroads into the American market. These saws represent a step up from typical American cabinet saws in terms of size, heft, features, and price. In general, these machines are larger, heavier, and more versatile than their traditional North American counterparts.

In its full form, a European tablesaw includes an integral sliding table, a riving knife, and a scoring blade. However, some manufacturers offer you the choice of the basic saw without the sliding table or scoring blade, which you can add later if you like. In addition to the saw's size and power, its sliding table is one of its biggest benefits, allowing you to crosscut large workpieces effortlessly. Sliding tables that extend all the way to the blade are called "format tables." Fairly narrow themselves, they include an attached outrigger that helps carry the workpiece. The optional sliding tables on a few saws stop short of the blade, creating a bit of workpiece drag on the table. Safety features are also a big part of the package. A

The optional sliding table on this saw doesn't extend all the way to the blade, inviting workpiece drag on the main table.

YOUR MONEY'S WORTH

In the tablesaw market, like any other (except maybe the stock market), you get what you pay for. Shelling out extra money buys you precision, durable parts, good fit and finish, and well-designed features—among other attributes. But keep in mind that manufacturers need to stay competitive. Don't expect perfection, even from a $5,000 saw, which may have slight flaws, ranging from cosmetic blemishes to minor design shortcomings that may require a bit of rectifying. That's okay. A "perfect" saw would probably cost more than you would want to pay anyway.

The protruding sliding table bed on a European saw necessitates working more from the side of the saw rather than from the front.

Panel Saws

Some industrial sliding tablesaws are designed primarily to handle sheet goods. These machines are real behemoths and can easily cost in the tens of thousands of dollars, depending on their size and features. They excel at handling large workpieces of any sort and are capable of performing any tablesaw function.

This behemoth panel saw makes cutting sheet goods a snap because of its 10-ft. table travel and other features.

Euro saw has a true riving knife and a blade shroud and dust port for safer cutting and easy breathing.

If you opt for a European saw, you'll have to learn to work a little differently from the way you do with a traditional cabinet saw. For one thing, the bed or rail that carries the sliding table projects out in front of the saw, forcing you to work to the side of the saw rather than from the front. But, by all accounts, it's not a difficult adjustment to make. Also, any jigs you may have made for a cabinet saw probably won't fit a Euro saw, and the arbor on some models won't accept a dado head, which may be an issue if you saw a lot of dadoes.

All in all, a European saw is a big step up from a traditional cabinet saw in terms of versatility, convenience, and safety. Figure on prices starting at about $2,500 for an entry-level saw. Better models can cost $5,000 or more.

A panel saw can rip a straight edge on a board. Pinch the board at its ends onto the sliding table and then push forward.

Some larger panel saws have a sliding table with as much as 10 ft. of travel, which can easily rip an entire 4×8 panel to desired width. Feeding even heavy panels is a simple matter of pushing the table forward—a real breeze. A long table also allows easy straight-line ripping of lumber. To make the cut, the board is simply mounted on the table and pinched at each end between hold-downs or perhaps just pressed against the crosscut fence at one end. Pushing the table forward carries the board past the blade, cutting a dead-straight edge quickly.

Obviously, these are not small-shop machines. You need plenty of cash for one and some serious shop real estate to accommodate such a large footprint.

NORTH AMERICAN "EUROPEAN" SAWS

Tablesaws with sliding tables, true riving knives, and integral scoring blades are no longer the sole province of European companies. For example, Canadian manufacturer General

International has released a tablesaw with all of these "European" features. I'm guessing we'll be seeing offerings like this from U.S. companies over time.

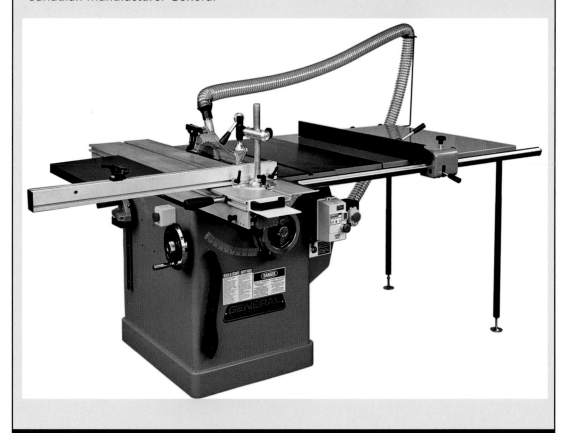

A combination machine includes a sliding tablesaw, a shaper, and a jointer (all shown here) as well as a planer and mortiser.

Positioning the sliding table fence in front of the workpiece allows crosscutting a full-size plywood panel on this combination machine.

A combo machine provides a lot of capability in one package, and its sliding table makes easy work of cross-cutting panels and large workpieces

Combination Machines

A combination machine may be a good choice for a serious woodworker who is pressed for shop space. These European beasts combine a tablesaw, shaper, jointer, planer, and mortiser into one basic package. A combo machine includes a sliding table for easy crosscutting of panels and large workpieces. In fact, by reversing the crosscut fence on the sliding table, it's possible to

crosscut a full sheet of plywood quickly and accurately.

Of course, there may be a bit of change-over time when switching from one operation to another, but it usually takes only about a minute. A combination machine might be a good choice if you're working in tight quarters and plan on buying a new jointer, planer, and shaper anyway. Don't worry that the individual machines are inferior because they're part of a combination tool. This isn't cheap stuff, underscored by the fact that a combination machine can cost you anywhere from $5,000 to $25,000, depending on quality, size, and features.

Saw Anatomy

Despite differences in size, the exteriors of most saws are remarkably similar. All have a base (whether open or closed), a table with miter gauge slots, handwheels for raising and tilting the blade, and a switch. Even the internal mechanisms share the same basic parts and operating principles. Let's take a look at the makeup of these machines, starting with the guts.

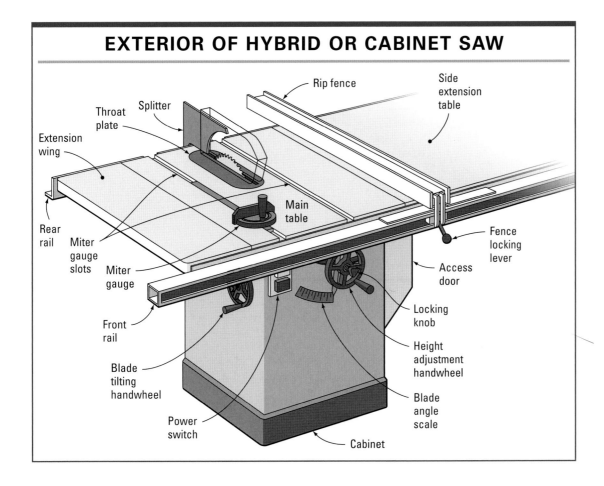

EXTERIOR OF HYBRID OR CABINET SAW

Rip fence

Side extension table

Throat plate

Splitter

Extension wing

Main table

Rear rail

Miter gauge slots

Miter gauge

Fence locking lever

Access door

Front rail

Locking knob

Height adjustment handwheel

Blade tilting handwheel

Blade angle scale

Power switch

Cabinet

Internal Mechanisms

Most tablesaws are *tilting-arbor* saws. This means the blade tilts to cut bevels while the table remains level. (Some older models had tilting tables, which have since fallen out of favor.) Regardless of manufacturer, the internal anatomy of most models is fairly consistent. Saws differ primarily in the size and heft of the components and in the way in which the motor trunnion brackets attach to the saw.

The motor carriage consists of a front and rear trunnion connected by either a substantial cast metal yoke (in most cabinet saws) or two connecting bars (in lighter-weight saws). Each slotted trunnion hangs from a mating trunnion bracket, which allows the motor

carriage to tilt. The front trunnion includes a sector gear that meshes with a worm gear on the end of the arbor-tilting handwheel shaft.

[TIP] Some of the part names may differ, depending on a manufacturer's particular nomenclature.

An arbor bracket that pivots off of the yoke (or bars) includes the blade arbor and its attendant bearings and pulleys. The sector gear section of the bracket meshes with the worm gear on the arbor-raising handwheel shaft to raise and lower the blade. On cabinet saws and hybrid saws, the motor mounts to a bracket that also connects to the yoke or bar assembly. All in all, it's really not a very complex mechanism. It's wise to

INTERNAL MECHANISMS (CABINET-SAW PARTS)

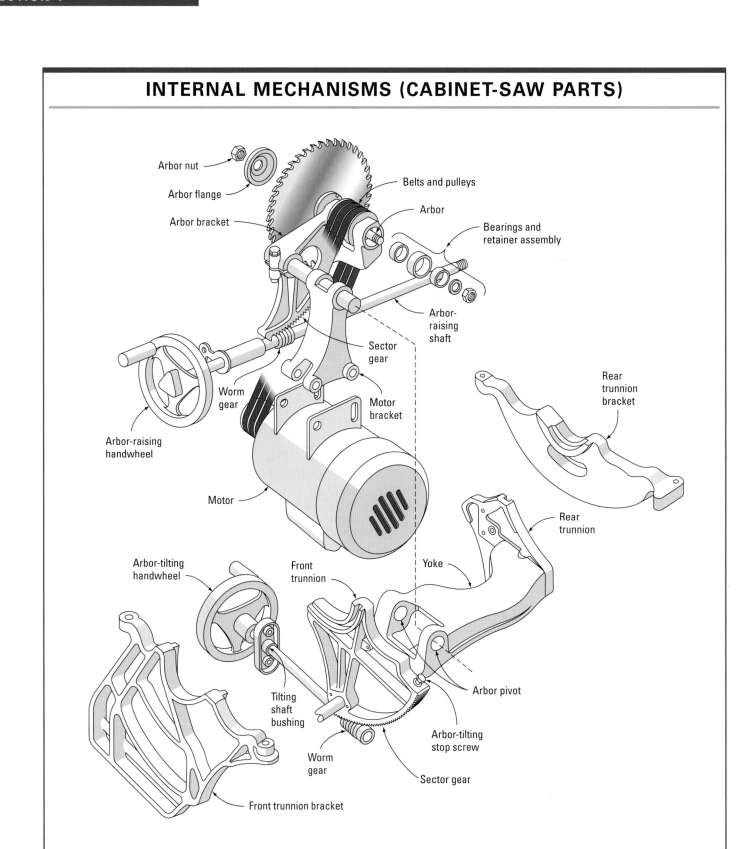

Arbor nut

Arbor flange

Arbor bracket

Belts and pulleys

Arbor

Bearings and retainer assembly

Arbor-raising shaft

Sector gear

Worm gear

Motor bracket

Arbor-raising handwheel

Rear trunnion bracket

Motor

Rear trunnion

Arbor-tilting handwheel

Front trunnion

Yoke

Arbor pivot

Tilting shaft bushing

Arbor-tilting stop screw

Worm gear

Sector gear

Front trunnion bracket

A side extension table converted into a router table allows your rip fence to do double-duty as the router fence.

A washer on the leading end of this miter gauge bar fits into the inverted T shape of the table slots, preventing the gauge from tipping when extended off of the saw.

WE WILL ONLY CUSTOM PLANE LUMBER FOR CUSTOMERS PURCHASING 500' OR MORE OF ONE THICKNESS AND SPECIES.

BOARD FOOTAGE
OUR LUMBER IS SOLD BY THE BOARD FOOT. ONE BOARD FOOT = 1"x12"x12". TO FIGURE OUT HOW MANY BOARD FEET ARE IN A PIECE OF LUMBER, MULTIPLY THE THICKNESS X THE WIDTH X THE LENGTH, AND DIVIDE THAT BY 12. (FOR EXAMPLE: 2"X6"X8'=96 DIVIDED BY 12=8 BOARD FEET) MULTIPLY THE BOARD FOOTAGE BY THE PRICE TO GET THE COST.

MEASUREMENT OF HARDWOOD LUMBER
OUR HARDWOOD LUMBER IS MEASURED ON THE NET BOARD FOOTAGE BASIS, AND NO ALLOWANCE FOR SHRINKAGE IS ADDED. PLEASE MAKE SURE WHEN COMPARING OUR PRICES THAT IT IS ALSO BASED ON MEASUREMENT AFTER KILN DRYING WITH NO ADD-ON BOARD FOOTAGE FOR SHRINKAGE.

RANDOM WIDTH AND RANDOM LENGTH SPECIFICATIONS
HARDWOOD LUMBER COMES RANDOM WIDTH AND RANDOM LENGTH. FOR EXAMPLE, HARDWOODS ARE NORMALLY PILED IN RANDOM LENGTHS 6'-16' LONG AND RANDOM WIDTHS 4" AND WIDER, AND 6" AND WIDER, ACCORDING TO THE N.H.L.A. INSPECTION RULES FOR THE GRADE AND SPECIES IN QUESTION.

PRICES PER BD/FT
FAS/SEL GRADE
UNLESS NOTED

HOURS
MONDAY - SATURDAY
8:00 - 4:00

*FSC CERTIFIED
"CERTIFIED AND NON-
CERTIFIED AVAILABLE

famili
nal m
manu
often
turers

Han
Excep
hand
the b
have
the w
whee
tilt-a
saws
comb
the f
lever

Tab
The
cut l
Sma
on p
for r
full-
dam
to n
deta
saws
with
tabl
exte
this

installing a router upside down beneath it, turning it into a router table. Your rip fence can then be pressed into service as your router table fence.

The tables on most contractor's saws, hybrid saws, and cabinet saws are about

Throat Plate

A saw's removable throat plate allows access for blade changing, splitter installation, and internal maintenance. For accurate sawing, it needs to be flat and level with the top of the saw table. Otherwise, it can impede

The underside of this aluminum throat plate is ribbed for strength. It includes four set-screws for leveling the plate to the saw table surface.

the travel of a workpiece or compromise critical cuts.

A stock throat plate is typically aluminum, with a ribbed underside and set screws that allow leveling it to the saw table. Its slot is fairly wide to allow tilting the blade. Unfortunately, this means that the workpiece fibers are unsupported on the underside of the cut, which can lead to exit tearout, especially when crosscutting. Narrow slices of wood can also get lodged in the gap. To beat those problems, it's great idea to buy or make a zero-clearance throat plate.

▶ See "Zero-Clearance Throat Plates" on p. 28.

Features to Consider

Some tablesaw features are bound to be of more importance to you, depending on the type of work you do or perhaps due to health or physical concerns. Here are a few things to weigh as you compare models.

Cutting Capacity and Power

Most woodworkers are well served by a decently powered 10-in. tablesaw, which will cut through stock nearly 3 in. thick with the blade at full height. (Don't expect a portable 10-in. saw to be happy with this task!) If you regularly work with very thick stock, consider springing for a 12-in. model, which will suit your purposes better. If you work with a lot of sheet goods or large stock, look for a large table as well as a fence with a 50-in. rip capacity or a large sliding table.

Ideally, your saw should have as much power as possible. However, every machine is designed to accommodate the type of motor it comes with. Don't even consider mounting a 3-hp motor on a contractor's saw, whose internal components are meant to withstand only a $1^{1}/_{2}$-hp motor. With hybrid saws, you're limited to a 2-hp motor. A 10-in. or 12-in. cabinet saw will accept a 3-hp or 5-hp motor. Realistically, a 3-hp motor handles most woodworking chores just fine. For a 12-in. saw cutting a lot of heavy stock, consider the larger motor.

Switches

A magnetic switch is a great safety feature because it shuts the switch off after a power interruption so the saw won't suddenly jump back to life when you restore the power. In addition, a large switch that can be turned off with a bump of the knee can be a real blessing in case of an emergency.

Miter Gauge

A miter gauge should slide in its slot easily but without side-to-side play. Better models have positively locking handles; a finely calibrated angle scale; and solid, adjustable stops for 90 degrees and 45 degrees. The body itself should be sturdy and attached firmly to the bar. It should have a couple holes for attaching an auxiliary fence; but if it doesn't, it's not a big deal to drill them yourself.

An oversize switch that can be shut down with the bump of a knee can save the day if letting go of your stock first would be a dangerous move.

The miter gauge should slide easily in its slots, with no side-to-side play.

Fence and Rails

The stock rip fences on most tablesaws used to be their Achilles' heel. The fence was usually cranky to adjust and rarely locked parallel to the blade, leading to errant cuts and increased risk of kickback. These days, new saws typically come outfitted with a solid, accurate, premium-quality fence. Most of these were originally designed as aftermarket fences and can be retrofit to almost any contractor's saw, hybrid saw, or cabinet saw, although not to a portable saw.

The first premium rip fence was invented in the late 1970s by Bill Biesemeyer. The Biesemeyer® fence eventually took the

▶ LEFT TILT VS. RIGHT TILT

Most manufacturers offer their tablesaws with a choice of right- or left-tilting blades. This has nothing to do with politics. It used to be that right-tilting saws were the norm, but this situation is changing. Manufacturers and woodworkers have come to realize that a left-tilting saw offers the advantage of comfortable, safe, accurate bevel ripping, especially of wide panels. Beveling with the fence to the right of the blade allows the bevel to ride above the tilted blade, as it should for safe, clean sawing. A couple of downsides: The first is that a left-tilting saw requires readjustment of your fence cursor and splitter when you change to a thin-kerf blade. The other is that crosscutting bevels using a sliding table traps the bevel under the blade.

▶ See "Ripping Bevels" on p. 130.

The classic Biesemeyer fence, with its simple, bulletproof T-square construction, has spawned numerous imitators.

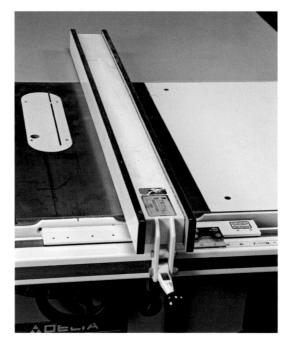

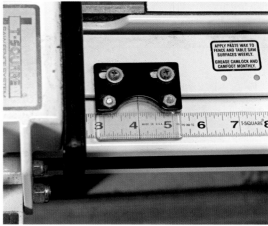

The cursor and scale on a Biesemeyer (or Biesemeyer-style) fence allows quick, accurate setting of the fence.

industry by storm and spawned a host of imitators. The body of the fence is a rectangular tube faced with plastic laminate–covered plywood. (Some Biesemeyer-style fences are faced with polyethylene plastic instead.) The body is welded to an angle-iron crossbar that rides on the front fence rail—also a rectangular tube. When the front lever is pushed down, a cam presses against the rail, securely locking the fence in position while maintaining its parallelism to the sawblade. An adjustable cursor on the crossbar hovers over a scale on the front rail, allowing quick, accurate settings to precise measurements. These fences don't lock to the system's rear rail, which serves only to support a side extension table.

[TIP] Many manufacturers offer a less expensive "home-shop" version of their fence. These are typically just as strong and accurate as their big brothers, just smaller.

Some other fence designs do lock onto a rear rail, which can be helpful if you often use fence-mounted featherboards. Some fences incorporate T-slots in the top or face for attaching hold-downs and other jigs, as shown in the top right photo on p. 94. Some fences include micro-adjusting mechanisms. One model even rides on pulley-guided wires.

One distinctively different model is the Delta Unifence®. Based on European rip fence design, the aluminum body can be adjusted fore and aft to create a "short fence," if desired. It can also be mounted in the low position for better push stick clearance or placed on the right side of its carriage for ripping with the fence to the left of the blade.

If you're still struggling with an old-style traditional fence, one of the best things you can do for your saw is to upgrade to a premium fence. When buying a new saw, you may not have a choice of fence systems, but it would be hard to go wrong with any of the available models these days.

Delta's Unifence can be mounted in either a high or a low position. The latter is better when working with thin stock and when extra push stick space is needed for ripping narrow pieces.

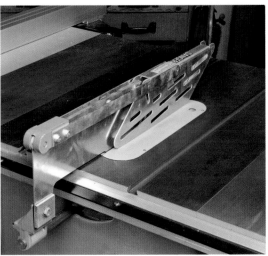 

The stock blade guard at left, which pivots off the rear end of the splitter plate, drops down over the sawblade in use. The splitter at right, bolts to a bracket inside the throat plate opening and to a rear bracket that bolts to a rod extending from the rear of the saw.

Splitters and Riving Knives

To prevent kickback, it's crucial that a table-saw be equipped with a splitter or riving knife to prevent the workpiece from contacting the rising rear teeth of the blade and flying back at the operator.

▶ See "What Causes Kickback?" on p. 71.

A splitter, like the stock unit on most saws sold in the United States for years, doesn't rise and fall with the blade, although it tilts with it. These splitters are a sort of three-part blade guard assembly that consists of the blade cover, the splitter, and a set of anti-kickback pawls. The cover and pawls attach to the splitter plate, which bolts to brackets on the saw.

A riving knife, on the other hand, rises, falls, and tilts with the blade while hugging its curvature to minimize any gap that might otherwise allow kickback. A true

A high-end sliding table saw includes a "true" riving knife, which hugs the blade curvature and sits just below the teeth at top dead center.

The hole at the top of this riving knife accommodates a removable blade cover (not shown).

riving knife sits just below the top of the blade, so it never has to be removed when cutting grooves or other non-through cuts. Some manufacturers include two interchangeable riving knives with their saws. One sits below the blade and one sits slightly above it, carrying a blade cover.

A riving knife is much safer and more convenient than a splitter. In fact, as

explained in Section 4, all saws sold in the United States will have to be outfitted with a riving knife by 2012 to gain UL (United Laboratories) approval, which is an essential safety assurance.

▶ See "Traditional Splitters Join the Dinosaurs" on p. 77.

Scoring Blade

A scoring blade is a small-diameter blade that sits in front of the main blade and spins in the opposite direction. It makes a shallow (about $1/32$-in.) preliminary *scoring* cut before the full cut is made by the main blade. The effect of this is to virtually eliminate any tearout, even in panels with delicate face veneers.

As you might expect, a scoring blade is standard issue on panel saws and some European saws. For other models, it's offered as an option. The blade can be adjusted

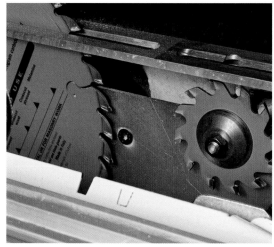

To eliminate tearout on plywood and other sheet goods, a small scoring blade makes a very shallow cut before a workpiece reaches the main blade.

side to side and dropped down out of play when desired. If you work with a lot of sheet goods, a saw with a scoring blade can save you lots of cleanup.

Dust Control

For the longest time, American manufacturers were fairly cavalier about incorporating decent dust control into tablesaws. Contractor's saws had no dust control at all, and the only concession made in cabinet saws was a dust port at the bottom of the cabinet. Hooked up to a dust collector, the port served only to evacuate the cloud of swirling dust inside the cabinet. Most of the heavy dust and chips simply settled to the bottom, eventually blocking the port unless cleaned out.

European saws include a ported shroud under the blade that can be hooked up to a dust collector. This design feature is now being incorporated into some American cabinet and hybrid saws. Many portables feature blade shrouds that can be hooked up to a shop vacuum. Although you can't expect to capture all the dust produced by a tablesaw, these internal features help. An overhead blade guard outfitted for dust collection also helps the situation.

▶ See Aftermarket Blade Guards" on p. 78.

Mobility

The ability to move a tablesaw around can be important if you're working in a small shop. Almost any saw can be accessorized with a commercial mobile base, but a few saws come with integral retracting casters. The beauty of integral casters is that, when retracted, the saw's cabinet sits firmly on the floor instead of on a raised platform, which never feels completely sturdy. Some European companies offer a "caster package" as an option for their saws. If I had to move my saw around a lot, I would definitely consider a model with integral casters.

▶ See "Mobile Bases" on p. 36.

Outfitting Your Shop for a Tablesaw

Whether you're bringing a tablesaw home for the first time or upgrading from a smaller model, you'll want to prepare your shop for it. To get the most from your saw, it will need to be well situated, well lit, and powered with the appropriate voltage.

Saw Placement

The most important consideration when placing your saw is allowing a stock feed zone around it. Most often, a tablesaw is centrally located in a shop. Ideally, you'll want at least 9 ft. of clearance in front of the blade and behind it, to allow comfortable ripping of sheet goods and 8-ft.-long lumber. If space is restricted, there's nothing wrong with threading stock through available doors and windows.

Allow as much room as possible to the left and right for crosscutting long pieces. If you must place the saw against a wall, make it the right side of the saw. Also keep stock flow in mind. There's a lot of back-and-forth stock movement between the jointer, planer, and tablesaw, so you'll want them relatively near each other. For safety and efficiency,

A safe, efficient tablesaw workstation includes an outfeed table as well as a nearby saw accessories cabinet.

include an outfeed table and a saw accessories cabinet as part of your tablesaw workstation, if space allows.

[TIP] Ideally, the saw operator should face the main shop door so as not to be startled from behind by an unexpected guest.

Electrical Needs

The universal motor on most portable saws runs only on standard 115v household current, so special shop wiring isn't an issue. However, the dual-voltage motors on contractor's saws and hybrid saws can be wired to run off of either 115v or 230v. It's definitely better to run these on 230v wherever possible because the motor runs more effi-

ciently, adding to its life and creating fewer circuit overloads. If you do your own electrical work (check with your local municipality to make sure this is legal), you know that it's usually not a big deal to install a 230v circuit in an electrical panel. (Use a 20-amp breaker for these motors.) If you're not sure of what you're doing, hire a qualified electrician.

Whether 115v or 230v, a saw should always have its own dedicated circuit that runs no other tools at the same time. Ideally, your power outlet should be nearby for convenient disconnection when changing blades. To prevent power loss, don't use an extension cord on a tablesaw. If you must, keep it as short as possible and make sure it's at least as heavy as the saw's power cord.

Lighting

To work with any kind of accuracy and efficiency, you must be able to see well. Make sure your tablesaw area enjoys good overall ambient light from windows and/or fluorescent fixtures. In addition, incandescent task lighting can be a real help, especially when ripping long stock that places you some distance from the saw. In that case, I train an overhead 100w flood lamp on my rip fence so I can keep a close eye on whether the stock stays against the fence as I cut.

Work Mats

If you spend a fair amount of time at your saw, you'll appreciate the value of a rubber mat underfoot. It helps prevent fatigue, especially on concrete floors, and aids in a solid, firm stance at the saw, which improves safety. Use a good mat with tapered edges that prevent tripping, and perhaps get one in a loud color to catch the eye. Stay away from cheap mats with blunt edges. You definitely don't want to trip while approaching the saw.

Shop Dust Control

A 1-hp single-stage dust collector rated at about 450 cfm will do a sufficient job of evacuating the dust from a cabinet saw. To maximize suction, use blast gates to close off any other ports coming in from other machines not in use. Also, keep the dust collector's upper bag from caking with dust, which impedes efficiency. Every time I empty my lower bag, I remove the upper one and take it outside. There, I turn it inside out, shake it violently, then beat it with a bench brush. Fun and effective!

An anti-fatigue floor mat in front of the tablesaw makes for comfort and a better stance. Avoid cheap mats with trip-prone squared edges like the one shown in the foreground here.

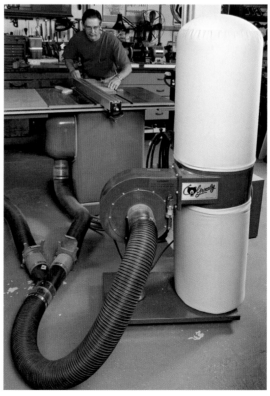

A typical 1½-hp dust collector works well at controlling tablesaw dust, as long as it's not pulling air from another machine at the same time.

The easiest way to control suction with multiple hoses is to install blast gates that can easily be opened and closed.

Craig Bentzley made his own ambient air cleaner from an attic fan, two high-efficiency home furnace filters, and a rheostat for controlling fan speed.

If you like, it's not difficult to make your own ambient air cleaner from a 14-in. attic fan, a couple of high-efficiency home furnace filters, and a motor rheostat for controlling fan speed.

Buying Used

Used saws can be a great value. Tablesaws don't have a lot of parts that can wear and don't break very easily. If you know what to look for, you can pick up a perfectly service-able saw for half the price of an equivalent new model. When you go to investigate a saw, bring along a basic tool kit, including screwdrivers, wrenches, a good straightedge, and an inspection flashlight.

The first thing to scrutinize on a used saw is the condition of the arbor and bearings. If noise or clunking indicates excessive wear, you may want to take a pass on the saw, particularly if it's an older model with difficult-to-replace parts. Use your straight-edge to make sure that the top is reasonably flat. Carefully check for cracked castings,

An ambient air cleaner hung from the ceiling sucks very fine ambient dust particles into its filter, cleaning the shop air.

Even a powerful dust collector connected to the saw can't corral all the dust a saw makes, especially the tiniest particles, which are the most harmful to your lungs. To cap-ture those, a lot of woodworkers install an overhead *ambient* air cleaner to draw the very fine dust into filters. These units are available in various sizes and price ranges.

▶ See "Resources" on p. 217.

Purchasing a used saw, such as this older model, can save you some money and afford you the opportunity to play with some classic American iron.

▶ See "Assess the Arbor Assembly" on p. 104.

missing parts, and excessive rust, which may indicate serious neglect. Operate the handwheels to check their full range, but don't fret too much about stiff movement due to gunk caked on the gears. The gears can be cleaned and lubricated.

Test the motor, listening for any screeching that may indicate worn bearings. But don't let that squash an otherwise good deal; motors can be replaced. Check the operation of the fence. If it's a traditional stock fence rather than a modern T-square type,

you might be able to use that fact to shave the asking price down a bit. You're probably going to want to replace it with a good aftermarket model anyway.

All in all, buying a used saw can be a great way to save yourself a few hundred bucks. But make sure to set aside at least a day to clean and tune it up.

Accessories

Zero-Clearance Throat Plates

Crosscut Sled

Other Accessories

To BRING OUT THE FULL capabilities of a tablesaw, you need to outfit it with the appropriate jigs, fixtures, and other helpers to hold and guide workpieces for specific cutting operations. In fact, the rip fence is nothing more than a jig that guides the workpiece in a straight line past the blade, while the miter gauge guides pieces for crosscutting and mitering. Without these "jigs," a tablesaw is pretty much useless, if not downright dangerous.

In this section, we'll take a look at various essential accessories for ripping, crosscutting, and mitering on the tablesaw. I'll discuss zero-clearance throat plates, aftermarket miter gauges, crosscut sleds, commercial sliding table add-ons, and feed supports.

Covering the entire arena of commercial offerings is beyond the scope of this book, but I'll show you a good representative sample of what's available these days. In addition, I'll provide step-by-step instructions for making some of these accessories yourself.

Of course there is also a wide range of tablesaw jigs for making joints and shaping pieces, but I'll cover those in Sections 10 and 11.

Zero-Clearance Throat Plates

One of the simplest and best improvements you can make to a saw is to switch out the stock throat plate for a zero-clearance throat plate, also called a *zero-clearance insert*. (Let's call it a ZCI for short.)

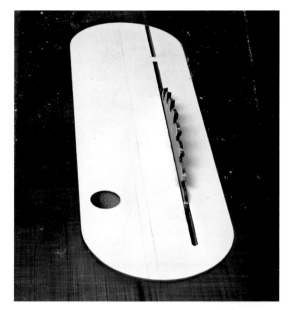

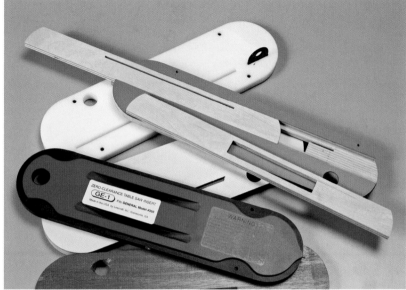

The slot on a zero-clearance throat plate comes right up to the blade, supporting the wood fibers for a cleaner cut and preventing narrow strips from falling into the saw.

The slot on a ZCI is made by the blade itself, which leaves virtually no gap between the sawteeth and the sides of the slot. This has a couple of benefits. For one, narrow off-cuts can't drop into the throat plate gap. But just as important, the wood fibers are fully supported on the exit side of the kerf, result-ing in cleaner cuts, particularly when cross-cutting. The only problem with a ZCI is that it prevents sawblade tilt, although most cutting is done at 90 degrees anyway. In any case, don't throw away your stock throat plate because you'll need it when making beveled cuts.

You'll want a variety of ZCI plates to suit various cutters, including standard and thin-kerf blades, dado blades, and perhaps molding heads. ZCI blanks are available commer-cially in a selection of materials, including polyethylene plastic, phenolic, and laminated plywood. These can be pricey, but don't worry, it's easy to make your own.

Zero-clearance throat plates are available com-mercially, or you can make your own from wood, plywood, or MDF covered with plastic laminate.

▶ See "Making a Zero-Clearance Throat Plate" on p. 38.

[TIP] Small, powerful rare-earth magnets stuck to your saw cabinet provide a great way to keep wrenches and other tools right at hand when you need them.

An auxiliary miter gauge fence that extends all the way to the blade lets you register your cutline against the end of the fence to easily and accurately set up the cut.

A section of aluminum T-track screwed into a groove in this auxiliary miter gauge fence allows lateral adjustment for supporting work right up to the blade.

This Accu-Miter® miter gauge from JDS includes an integral tape rule, a flip stop, a telescoping fence, and a stock hold-down.

Improving a Stock Miter Gauge

The typical stock miter gauge that comes with a tablesaw doesn't offer much crosscutting capacity or capability due to the size of its fence. Fortunately, you can easily add an auxiliary fence to increase the workpiece bearing surface. Also, if you extend the fence all the way to the blade, its end will serve as a reference for your cutline while backing up the cut to minimize exit tearout. To improve accuracy, glue 220-grit sandpaper to the fence face to prevent workpiece shift during cutting.

Make the auxiliary fence from a stable, straight-grained piece of wood that you have dressed straight and square. You can simply screw it to your miter gauge head, but a better approach is to inset T-track into the rear face and attach the fence with cap screws. This allows repositioning the fence laterally to re-trim a chewed-up end or to provide support closer to the blade when angling the jig for miter cuts. You can also add T-track to the top of the fence to accept flip stops if you like.

➤ For tips on installing the T-track, see "Finger Joint Jig" on p. 180.

Aftermarket Miter Gauges

A number of manufacturers make great aftermarket miter gauges that work a whole lot better than stock units. Some include fences that adjust laterally and that telescope out for greater capacity when registering multiple cuts against a stop. Most include flip stops for repetitive cutting of multiples, and some include a stock hold-down.

A good aftermarket miter gauge isn't cheap, but it's terrifically convenient for crosscutting and mitering small- to moderate-size pieces, especially if you don't have a crosscut sled. I've tried various models of aftermarket miter gauges and found that, although features vary, every one has been very accurate, convenient, and a vast improvement over a stock miter gauge.

Crosscut Sleds and Miter Sleds

Even a good aftermarket miter gauge is too small to provide solid support for crosscutting wide panels and long workpieces. To make the most of your saw's crosscutting capabilities, you need a way to feed large, long stock safely and accurately. If your saw doesn't include a sliding table, a crosscut sled is the next best solution. A sled rides in the saw's miter gauge slots and provides solid support and backup for big workpieces. Because the workpiece rides on the sled panel, you eliminate almost all possibility of an inaccurate cut caused by the workpiece shifting its position along the fence as can frequently happen with a miter gauge.

A double-runner crosscut sled runs in both miter gauge slots and has a fence that's fixed at 90 degrees to the blade for perfectly square cuts every time. Because the sled panel extends to both sides of the blade, offcuts are carried safely past the blade instead of dropping down onto the table after the cut. Another important advantage to a double-runner sled is that the saw kerf in the sled panel serves as a zero-clearance throat plate, supporting the wood fibers right up to the blade and minimizing exit tearout.

A shopmade crosscut sled that rides in your saw's miter gauge slots is just the ticket for crosscutting panels and other large workpieces.

A well-made frame miter sled will give you perfectly mating 45-degree miters every time.

For cutting 45-degree frame miters, it's hard to beat a dedicated sled with two fixed fences set up at 45 degrees to the blade. Just position the mating workpieces against the adjacent fences in their assembled relationship for a perfect 90-degree miter joint.

▶ For information on building the sled, see "Frame Miter Sled" on p. 48.

Commercial Sleds

A few commercially made crosscut sleds are available in case you don't want to build your own. Better models include flip stops, hold-downs, and perhaps even a blade guard.

Commercially available crosscut sleds like this hefty model from Woodhaven® can be adapted to fit almost any contractor's saw, hybrid saw, or cabinet saw.

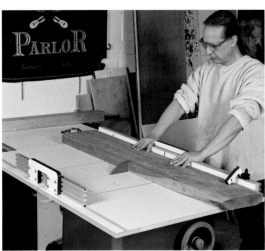

Shopmade Sleds

It's not hard to make your own crosscut sled. I have several in different sizes. Over the years, I have refined my design to create a sled that's as lightweight as possible while maintaining strength and maximum cutting height. My design also allows you to easily and accurately set the sled fence square to the blade, which is typically the most troublesome aspect of building a sled. The sled can also be outfitted to accept an extension bar with a stop block—a big step toward accuracy and convenience, especially when cutting multiples.

A crosscut sled with a wide slot allows you to cut dadoes safely and accurately on long and/or narrow case sides and other workpieces.

You can make crosscut sleds in any convenient size, small or large. However, if you

▶ See "Making a Crosscut Sled" on p. 41.

▶ See "Sled Extension Bar" on p. 45.

build standard-size cabinets, make sure you have a sled with at least a 24-in. crosscut capacity. I have three large sleds, one of which I use for sawing dadoes in narrow cabinet sides.

Aftermarket Sliding Tables

As discussed in Section 1, sliding tablesaws are a real boon when crosscutting sheet goods and other large workpieces. As an alternative to these expensive saws, a few manufacturers offer sliding tables that can be retrofit to many standard tablesaws. These add-on units are available in various sizes, with larger models providing the ability to crosscut full-size sheet goods. The table rides on wheels and carries the workpiece effortlessly past the blade, saving you the work of shoving it across the table and possibly causing a miscut if the piece shifts as you struggle to balance and support it.

An aftermarket sliding table consists of a metal panel or framework that attaches to a carrier framework that you fix to your saw. Rollers under the table frame carry the load, making it easy to push even heavy workpieces. Note, however, that these tables don't extend all the way to the blade as do the integral "format" sliding tables built into European-style saws. The fence can be mounted at the front or rear of the table, and may be angled to make miter cuts, even on wide panels. Normally, the fence lives at the front of the table, where it's used as sort of an oversize miter gauge. Mounting it at the rear allows crosscutting very wide panels. Some sliding tables are fairly narrow and don't provide much bearing surface, in which case you'll need to provide outfeed support when crosscutting long stock.

The Excalibur® sliding table affixes to the side of a saw for carrying large workpieces effortlessly. (The outfeed rollers to the left are not part of the sliding table system.)

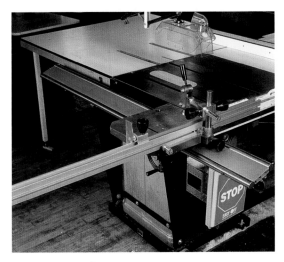

The Robland® add-on sliding table doesn't take up a lot of floor space, but the small table requires side-feed support for long workpieces.

Mounting an aftermarket sliding table usually means removing your saw's left-hand extension table. No problem. However, it also means either cutting off a section of your rip fence rail or shifting the rail to the right to accommodate the movement of the sliding table. In my experience, installing an add-on table and fussing it into perfect alignment can easily take a day or so. Once it's set up, though, it should hold its alignment well as long as you don't accidentally roll a heavy compressor against one of the legs or move your saw across the shop.

At $500 to about $1,000, these units aren't cheap, but if you often work with large sheet goods, a sliding table can save you a lot of time and trouble. Just make sure you have the shop real estate to accommodate it. Fitting a sliding table to a saw that has a 50-in.-capacity rip fence can extend the saw's total footprint to about 9 ft. wide . Finally, as good as these aftermarket sliding tables are, don't kid yourself that any of them will be as smooth, precise, or durable as the integral sliding tables built into European-style sliding tablesaws.

▶ See "European Saws" on p. 11.

Extension Tables

I consider side extension tables and outfeed tables to be crucial tablesaw accessories. If you don't have a side extension table that reaches under your rip fence at its maximum capacity, workpieces can sag down under the fence. Plus, a side table serves as a great holding area for stacks of work to be cut. Many woodworkers also mount a router in their side extension table to save shop space, which also allows use of the rip fence as a router table fence. Side extension tables are available commercially, but it's easy to build one yourself. Just make sure that its front-to-back depth matches your saw table depth for an exact fit between your rip fence rails. Otherwise, you risk bending the rails and cocking your rip fence on wide cuts.

Not every shop can accommodate a large outfeed table, but even a small table is a bonus. An outfeed table will prevent small workpieces from falling damaged to the floor after a rip cut and will help support long pieces. If you're cramped for space, consider devising an outfeed table that hinges to your saw, allowing it to be dropped down when not needed.

I find that a freestanding outfeed table that tucks up against the saw provides the best of all worlds. It's large enough to support an 8-ft.-long panel at the end of the cut and does double-duty as an assembly table. It's easy to make, and the lag screw feet allow fine height adjustment for aligning the top to your saw table. An added advantage of a freestanding table is that it can be pulled away from the saw to create a saw channel for safely crosscutting large panels.

▶ See the top right photo on p. 156.

Using your side extension table as a router table can be a real shop space saver. Thick boards attached to your rip fence allow you to bury the bit behind the fence face.

OUTFEED TABLE

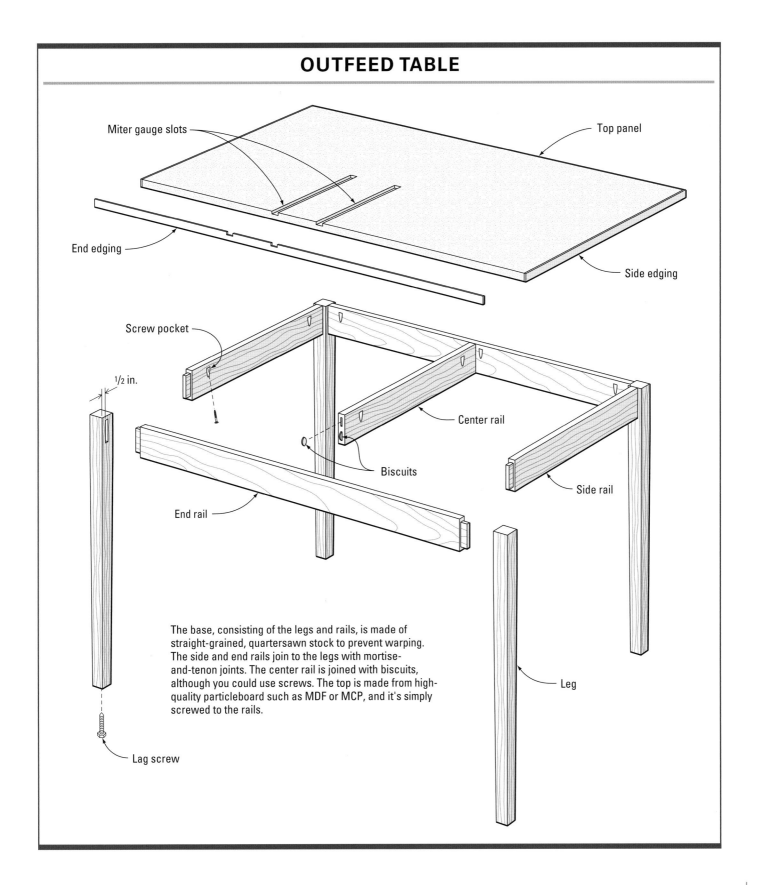

Miter gauge slots

Top panel

End edging

Side edging

Screw pocket

1/2 in.

Center rail

Biscuits

Side rail

End rail

The base, consisting of the legs and rails, is made of straight-grained, quartersawn stock to prevent warping. The side and end rails join to the legs with mortise-and-tenon joints. The center rail is joined with biscuits, although you could use screws. The top is made from high-quality particleboard such as MDF or MCP, and it's simply screwed to the rails.

Leg

Lag screw

A large freestanding outfeed table offers plenty of support for big workpieces and doubles as an assembly table.

You can make a quick infeed support stand by clamping a panel to a sturdy sawhorse.

Portable Feed Supports

Close quarters may not allow for a dedicated outfeed table. And even if you have space, there will be times when you need to set up infeed support for long pieces or side support for wide panels. In those cases, you'll need portable support stands. Ideally, you'll want a sure-footed stand that allows fine height adjustment.

There is no shortage of commercial models or designs for shop-built stands. For a quick infeed support, you can simply clamp a panel to a sawhorse. However, a good outfeed support stand will include a ramp of some sort to guide a drooping board up onto the stand. One popular commercial model has a plat-

form that tilts downward a bit to catch the board and then flattens out as the board travels over it.

[TIP] A stand with a cylindrical roller can be troublesome. A roller that isn't set perfectly perpendicular to your sawblade can steer the stock away from the fence during ripping operations.

Mobile Bases

In cramped quarters, one of the best things you can do is outfit your tablesaw with a mobile base. That way you can roll the machine out of the way to gain more floor space, perhaps to assemble a cabinet, or

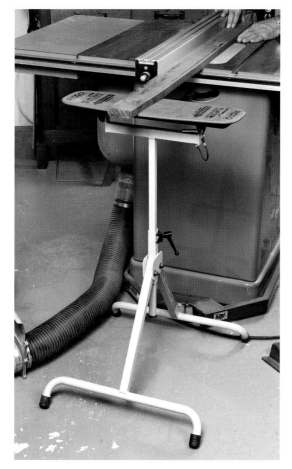

The Ridgid® support stand pivots downward toward the saw to catch the approaching board and then levels out. It can also be locked in a horizontal position when desired.

I'll admit it, I'm old school when it comes to many jigs, fixtures, and accessories. I tend to build them myself if at all possible. In over 30 years of woodworking, I've made plenty that work great. However, if you're just starting to develop your woodworking chops, you may wonder whether to buy or build. My advice is to try making any accessory you think is within your abilities. Good plans are available in this book and elsewhere. And there's nothing wrong with devising your own approaches. You'll build your woodworking skills while learning how to problem solve.

That said, sometimes it makes more sense to buy a good commercial product. You'll pay for it, but you'll get accuracy, durability, and functionality right off the bat. A commercial accessory allows you to get on with building cabinets, furniture, or whatever else you want to make in your shop.

center the saw in your shop when maximum infeed and outfeed area are needed.

There are quite a few commercial mobile bases to choose from, or you can make your own using a set of heavy-duty casters. Companies like HTC® offer a wide range of bases for specific sizes of saws.

▶ For buying information, see "Resources" on p. 217.

Tablesaw mobility is a must in many cramped shops. Manufacturers like HTC offer sturdy bases for a wide variety of saws and other shop machines.

A

Making a Zero-Clearance Throat Plate

In my experience, some of the flattest, most stable zero-clearance throat plates are made from ½-in.-thick MDF (medium-density fiberboard) covered on both sides with plastic laminate, which also provides a low-friction surface. The laminated MDF is just thicker than 9/16 in., making for a nearly perfect fit in the throat plate recess of my Unisaw. Suit the thickness to your own saw.

Cut an MDF blank about ½ in. wider and longer than your saw's throat plate recess. Also cut two pieces of plastic laminate the same size. Apply the plastic laminate to both sides with contact cement, pressing it firmly in place with a roller or bullnose board **(A)**.

Rip just enough from one edge of the blank to flush up the laminate and the MDF. Then mark the blank for width. A snug side-to-side fit in the recess is critical, so mark directly from the insert opening, then make a nibble cut and test the fit **(B)**. After ripping the blank to width, use the stock throat plate to mark the rounded ends **(C)**. Drill a finger access hole. Bandsaw or jigsaw a bit proud of the lines, finish up with a disc or belt sander, and test the fit with the sawblade removed.

You can install leveling screws or simply rout away the areas of the underside that contact the metal tabs at the bottom of the recess **(D)**. If you overcut, just shim with masking tape.

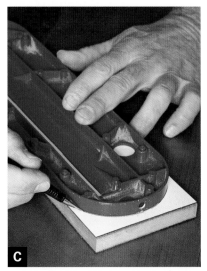

B

C

D

VARIATION

[VARIATION] Rather than sanding the curved ends of each plate, you can finesse one perfectly fitting "master" blank and dedicate it as a template-routing pattern. Attach it to another rough-bandsawn blank with double-sided tape or hot-melt glue, and finish up the curves using a flush-trimming bit in your router table.

Slotting a Throat Plate

To cut the slot with a standard blade, first back off the height-adjustment screws on your stock throat plate, then put it in place. This will create a shallow recess into which you can place your throat plate blank **(A)**. Clamp a strong, straight beam across the blank to one side of the blade location, and then slowly raise the blade until it just peeks through the surface **(B)**. Lower the blade, remove the stock plate, and install the zero-clearance blank. Again, clamp it down with the beam, and slowly raise the blade to complete the slot **(C)**. Finish up by cutting the splitter slot with a jigsaw **(D)**.

On many saws, the teeth of an installed blade reach nearly to the saw table surface, which prevents a zero-clearance insert from fully seating in the recess in order to cut the blade slot. The easiest approach is to begin the cut with a smaller blade, such as the outer blade from a stack dado that matches the tooth width of your standard blade. Install the dado blade, clamp the throat plate in its recess, then raise the blade until it just breaks the surface of the plate. Replace the small blade with a standard blade to complete the cut, again with the throat plate clamped down.

➤ See "Dado Heads" on p. 60.

[VARIATION] You can make a simple hold-down for slotting plates. Just grind opposing flats on a ⅜-in.-dia. barbless T-nut so it slides in a miter gauge slot, then make a simple wooden bridge with a center hole to accommodate a short section of ⅜-in.-dia. all-thread with a wing nut.

B

C

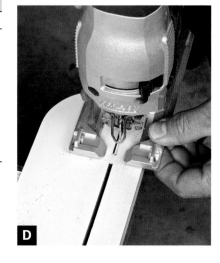
D

VARIATION

A

B

C

D

E

Throat-Plate Leveling Screws

The best way to level a throat plate is with adjustable setscrews that are accessible from the top side of the plate. They're easy to install in wood, MDF, or plastic and allow for fine height adjustment when a throat plate or saw top expands or contracts over the seasons. Allen-head setscrews are ideal for the job. For the typical throat plate, ¼-20 by ½-in.-long setscrews work nicely.

To install them you'll need a ¼-20 tap and a handle, both commonly available at hardware stores for a few bucks **(A)**. Using a ³⁄₁₆-in. bit, drill holes in the appropriate locations on your throat plate **(B)**. Use the tap to cut the threads for the setscrews **(C)**. If you haven't used a tap before, don't worry. It's as easy as keeping the tap relatively plumb while applying good downward force for the first ¼ in. or so. After that, you just turn the handle to finish cutting the threads. There is no need to use thread-cutting oil as you would when tapping a hole in a piece of metal. Just be sure to thread completely past the taper at the end of the tap **(D)**. Install the setscrews using an Allen wrench, and you're done **(E)**.

Making a Crosscut Sled

This crosscut sled is sized to accommodate 24-in.-wide panels, meaning it will handle most typical plywood cabinetry work. Size your sled as desired. Just make sure that it will overhang the left side of your saw by at least 1½ in. The ends of the brace and fence are stepped down to reduce the weight. The left end of the fence is higher to accommodate an extension bar with a stop block.

[TIP] Make sure your blade is precisely aligned with the saw's miter gauge slots before making a sled. Aligning it afterward will probably require resetting the sled fence for square cuts.

Begin by making the parts. Saw the panel from good-quality ½-in.-thick hardwood plywood. Mill the stock for the fence and brace from a stable hardwood like mahogany. Dress the fence straight and square and make sure that its bottom edge is square to its inner face. Saw the ⅛-in. by ⅛-in. rabbet in the bottom front edge for chip clearance, then lay out the shape on the brace and fence, centering the humps over the blade slot locations. Saw the pieces to shape with a jigsaw or bandsaw **(A)**, then rout the top edges with a ¼-in. roundover bit for comfort.

Mill hardwood runners to fit in the miter gauge slots. They should fit the slots snugly from side to side but be slightly shallower so they don't rub on the bottom of the slots. Also make the guard block, orienting the grain vertically for a long grain to long grain glue joint with the fence.

Attach the brace to the panel with countersunk screws, avoiding the blade's path **(B)**. Place the runners in their slots, shimming them so they're flush with the tabletop, then place the panel on top of them. For shims, use plastic laminate, dimes, or whatever works. Bring the rip fence

(text continues on p. 42)

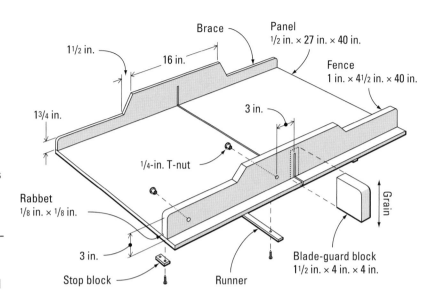

Brace — Panel ½ in. × 27 in. × 40 in. — Fence 1 in. × 4½ in. × 40 in. — 1½ in. — 16 in. — 1¾ in. — 3 in. — ¼-in. T-nut — Grain — Rabbet ⅛ in. × ⅛ in. — 3 in. — Stop block — Runner — Blade-guard block 1½ in. × 4 in. × 4 in.

A

B

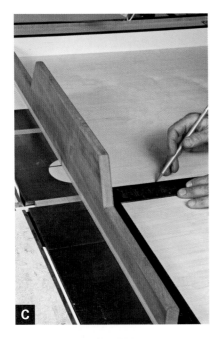

C

D

E

F

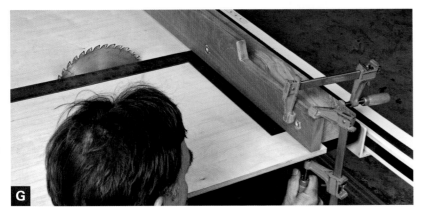

G

over against the side of the panel, and use it to help position the panel in relation to the blade. Make sure that the left side of the sled overhangs the table by about 1½ in. Then mark the runner centerlines on top of the panel **(C)**.

Drive 1-in. brads through the panel into the runners, leaving the heads proud for removal later. Then flip the sled upside down and attach the runners from underneath with countersunk flat-head screws **(D)**. Place the sled back into its slots, and trim the edges of the runners as necessary to create an easy, sliding fit with no side-to-side play. A shoulder plane or scraper works great for this **(E)**. However, you could also use a sanding block or scrape the runners using a sharp chisel. To help determine the spots that need to be removed, I rub the edges of the miter gauge slots with a wide-lead carpenter's pencil, which will leave graphite residue on any high areas.

Using a drill press, bore the stepped holes for the ⁵⁄₁₆-in.-dia. T-nuts in the face of the fence, and install the T-nuts **(F)**. (The depth of the counterbore may vary from that shown, depending on the length of the T-nut sleeves, the exact thickness of your fence, and the length of the studs on the knobs you use to attach the extension bar you'll make later.) With the fence inset ¾ in. from the front edge of the panel, attach it with a single screw at the far right end. Clamp the left end to the panel. If there is any slight bow to the fence, clamp a strong, jointed board to it to make it dead flat.

Raise the blade about 2 in. above the table and cut most of the way across the panel, stopping a couple of inches shy of the fence. Using an accurate square, adjust the fence until it is perpendicular to the kerf you just cut. Then tightly clamp the end of the fence to the panel **(G)**. Make a test crosscut using a wide piece of scrap that is about as long as the fence and that has abso-lutely parallel edges **(H)**. After making the cut, flip one of the halves upside down (marked "B" here) and butt the sawn edges together with the long edges against the fence **(I)**. If the ends meet per-fectly, the cut is square. If not, adjust the angle of the fence a bit and try again. When you're happy, screw the fence to the panel.

For safety, the sled should stop when the top of the blade meets the inside face of the fence. If using an outfeed table, you can simply make its miter gauge slots short enough to stop the sled's travel at the proper point. Alternatively, you can secure a flathead machine screw through the overhanging edge of the sled, locating it so it butts against a stop block screwed to the edge of the saw table **(J)**. This may require you to drill holes for a bolt or two through the side of the metal saw table. While you may be hesitant to make such a modification to your saw, it is well worth the effort for the safety it affords.

Attach the blade guard, gluing its long-grain edge to the fence. Make sure it's square to the fence because it serves as registration for the exten-sion bar **(K)**. Finish up by waxing the bottom of the sled for easy travel **(L)**.

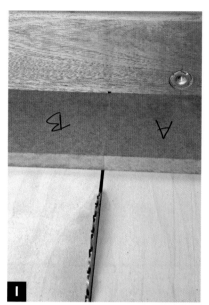

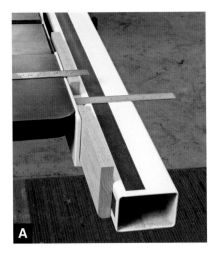

A

B

C

D

E

Crosscut-Sled Support Arm

The only problem with a large crosscut sled is that it tends to tip off the front of the saw when you're preparing for a cut. You can use an auxiliary stand for a support, but a less intrusive approach is to craft a short support that cantilevers off the front of the saw.

Like many woodworkers, I have a Biesemeyer fence. I've found that a simple three-piece wooden support works nicely. It consists of a wooden arm that lays across the fence's guide tube while dadoed into a crosspiece that fits snugly between the tube and the fence mounting rail. A cleat on the rear of the crosspiece presses against the underside of the tablesaw wing, locking the unit in place. This design can be modified to fit many similar saw/fence combinations.

Make the crosspiece about 16 in. long and just thick enough to slide between the fence tube and its mounting rail. If necessary, round over the bottom edge to seat the piece against the face and the bottom of the L-shaped rail. Trim the top edge to be just a hair below the tabletop, then cut a 3-in.-wide dado whose bottom sits flush with the top of the guide tube **(A)**. Locate the dado about 6 in. in from the outer end of the crosspiece. Make the 12-in.-long support arm so it fits snugly in the dado **(B)**, but don't fasten it yet.

Next, make the cleat that bears against the underside of the saw. Mine is ⅞ in. by 11 in. by 2½ in., but suit your particular tablesaw wing, making sure that the cleat bears solidly against the underside edge of the wing. Notch the long edge to accommodate the fence rail, with 4 in. or 5 in. solidly contacting the wooden crosspiece **(C)**. Holding the cleat in place, mark its location on the crosspiece **(D)**. Finally, glue and screw the parts together and round over the corners of the arm **(E)**.

Sled Extension Bar

You can outfit your sled with an extension bar and stop block that allow for efficient, accurate cutting of multiples. Make the bar from ¾-in.-thick hardwood that's 2¾ in. wide and any length you like. (Mine is 60 in.) Although you could simply clamp the bar to your sled fence, clamps can be a bit cumbersome and impede cutting of thick stock. This bar quickly attaches with a couple of 1½-in. male clamping knobs (available from Lee Valley Tools®; part #00M55.21), threaded into the sled fence's T-nuts from behind **(A)**.

To locate the knob holes in the bar, begin by clamping the bar to the rear of the sled fence, with the end of the bar butted firmly against the side of the blade guard. Next, make a drill guide by using the drill press to bore a ¼-in.-dia. hole through the edge of a piece of squared scrap stock at least 1 in. wide. You'll insert a ¼-in.-dia. brad point drill bit through the guide and T-nut to locate the drilling centers in the extension bar **(B)**. Holding the guide in place over the hole, insert the bit and twist it by hand while pressing against the extension bar **(C)**. Remove the extension bar and use the drill press to bore a 5⁄16-in.-dia. hole through it at each location.

To keep the knobs on the bar, drill a counterbore on the inside face of the bar to accept a rubber O-ring or other keeper **(D)**. (I drilled holes in thick rubber scraps, then cut them to size. Not pretty, but effective.)

A

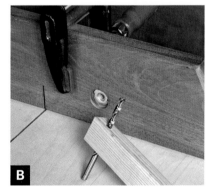

B

C

D

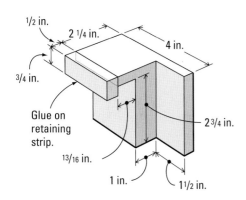

1/2 in.
2 1/4 in.
4 in.
3/4 in.
Glue on retaining strip.
2 3/4 in.
13/16 in.
1 in.
1 1/2 in.

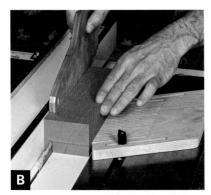

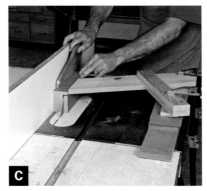

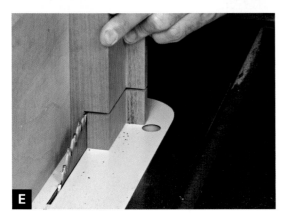

Quick-Set Stop Block

You can clamp a square stop block to the extension fence, but it's troublesome to square it up to the bar so the block butts firmly against the square end of a workpiece. Making minor adjustments with a simple square block can also be fussy. This custom stop block does a much better job because it hangs squarely in place on the bar for easy adjustment and clamping. Also, a large rabbet cut into the end of the block can overlap the sled fence when necessary to set a stop block at the very end of the fence **(A)**.

The stop block isn't hard to make. Begin with a 2¼-in. by 3¼-in. block of wood about 10 in. long for initial safe handling. Lay out and cut a ¹³⁄₁₆-in. by 2¾-in. rabbet along its length. Make the ¾-in.-deep cut first, using a featherboard for safety **(B)**. Making the remaining tall cut might be a bit dicey without help, so set up a tall fence and a raised featherboard to keep the piece against the fence **(C)**.

Next, lay out the 1-in. by 1½-in. rabbet on the end of the block. Saw the shoulder cut first, resting the previously sawn rabbet on a piece of dressed scrap for stability **(D)**. Make the cheek cut using a tenoning jig **(E)**. Glue a ½-in. by ¾-in. retaining strip to the rear edge of the stop block **(F)**. Finish up by crosscutting the block to about 4 in. long.

Auxiliary Tall Fence

This tall fence provides workpiece support when you're sawing panels on edge and allows the attachment of fence-mounted featherboards and sacrificial faces. Mine is 8 in. tall, and made from ¾-in.-thick MDF, but you could use good-quality plywood or other panel material, as long as it's flat.

Begin by sawing the 8-in.-wide face panel to a length about 2 in. longer than your fence. To make the cross panel, first determine the exact width of your fence by measuring between two squares placed on opposite sides **(A)**. Cut the strip for the top panel, including enough overage to make the front and back caps from the same piece. To determine the height of the rear leg, lay the top panel on the fence, measure down to the table-top, and add ¹⁄₁₆ in. for clearance. Cut the rear leg to this width.

Temporarily clamp the pieces together on the fence. There should be no side-to-side play, but you should be able to lift the assembly upward without undue effort **(B)**. With the unit still in place, measure for the height of the end caps, then cut them from the excess length of the top panel. Make sure the caps are dead square. Afterward, crosscut the long pieces to final size.

Biscuit-join the pieces **(C)**. (Screws or nails tend to split the edges of MDF—if you have to go this route, be sure to drill generous pilot holes.) Glue the end caps to the top panel, carefully aligning their edges. Glue on the rear leg, then attach the face panel after predrilling for a few counterbored screws that will serve as clamps **(D)**. Check to see if the assembled unit is square to your saw table **(E)**. If necessary, rip a bit off of the appropriate bottom edge to correct any fence tilt **(F)**. I finish up by applying plastic laminate to the face for durability and reduced friction.

▶ See "Applying Plastic Laminate" on p. 50.

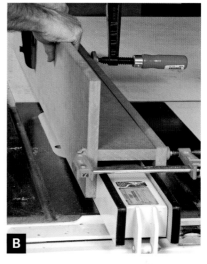

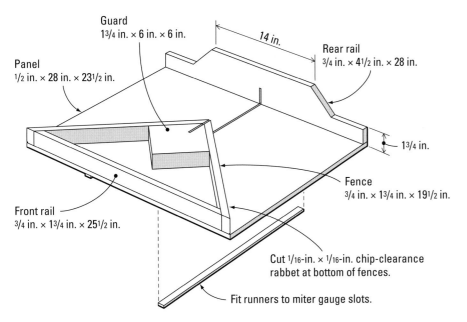

Guard
1¾ in. × 6 in. × 6 in.

Panel
½ in. × 28 in. × 23½ in.

14 in.

Rear rail
¾ in. × 4½ in. × 28 in.

1¾ in.

Fence
¾ in. × 1¾ in. × 19½ in.

Front rail
¾ in. × 1¾ in. × 25½ in.

Cut 1/16-in. × 1/16-in. chip-clearance rabbet at bottom of fences.

Fit runners to miter gauge slots.

Frame Miter Sled

This sled will allow you to miter the ends of frame pieces as wide as 6 in. The beauty of this design is that as long as the fences are mounted at precisely 90 degrees to each other, your miters will be perfect every time, even if the fences don't meet the blade at exactly 45 degrees. Just cut your miters in the same relationship to each other as they'll be when assembled. The braces along the front and rear edges help keep the sled's base flat, which is important for accurate cuts (A). To this end, I used nine-ply ½-in.-thick hardwood plywood for the base, as it tends to stay flatter than some other sheet materials.

Cut the parts as shown in the drawing, dressing everything straight, flat, and square. The runners should slide easily in your saw's miter gauge slots, but with no side-to-side play. Make them 1/16 in. thinner than the slot depth so they won't drag on the bottom. To reduce weight, shape the rear rail, rounding its edges for comfort. Miter the ends of each fence at 45 degrees, then cut a 1/16-in. by 1/16-in. chip-clearance rabbet into the bottom face of each fence piece. Saw the guard block absolutely square to ensure that the fences will attach to it at exactly 90 degrees.

Place the runners in their slots, shimming them with a few dimes. Mark for the saw kerf at the center of the panel. With your rip fence against the panel, align the cutline with the blade teeth and lock your saw's rip fence in place to register the panel's location.

Mark the runner centerlines across the panel, then drive a few small nails through the panel into the runners, leaving the heads proud (B). Upturn the sled, and attach the runners with countersunk flat-head screws (C). Scrub the sides of your miter gauge slots with a wide-lead carpenter's pencil, then test the runner's fit in the grooves.

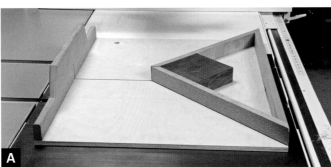

A

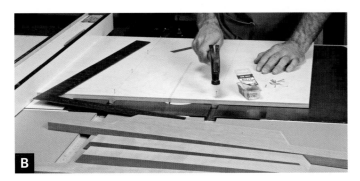

B

C

The pencil graphite will mark any high spots, which can be removed with a shoulder plane or cabinet scraper **(D)**.

Clamp the fences to the guard block on a flat surface, and drill and countersink for screws, avoiding the blade path **(E)**. Then glue and screw them together. Lay the fence/block assembly in its location on the sled, and mark where its nose intersects the sled's centerline. Saw to that point **(F)**. With the saw unplugged, raise the blade to full height, and place a 45-degree triangle against the blade, making sure it's flat against the blade plate. Extend an accurate straightedge from the triangle to your layout line and carry the line outward **(G)**. Align the fence assembly to this mark, with the nose centered on the panel kerf, and clamp it in place **(H)**.

Turn the jig over, and screw the fence/block assembly to the sled, avoiding the blade path. I used 1⅝-in. drywall screws, countersinking them. Also fit the front brace and screw it and the rear brace to the panel **(I)**. Raise your blade a couple of inches, and saw through the rear rail and just into the front ends of the fence. It's okay if the blade doesn't perfectly bisect the center of the fence miter. Finish up by applying fine sandpaper to the fence faces. Make sure to keep it above the chip-clearance rabbet. I use spray adhesive, after masking off the surrounding areas.

▶ **For instructions on using the sled, see "Frame Miters with Miter Sled" on p. 192.**

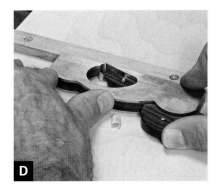

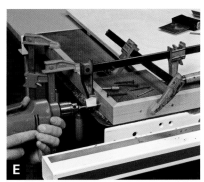

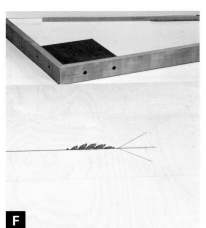

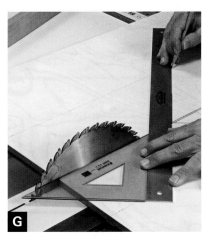

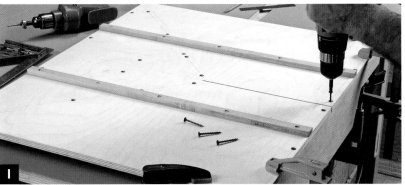

A

B

C

D

E

Applying Plastic Laminate

Many jigs, such as an auxiliary tall fence, benefit from a facing of plastic laminate, which protects the surface and reduces friction from work-pieces. Plastic laminate (two brand names are Formica® and Wilsonart®) is available at home supply centers, but you may be able to pick up scraps from a local cabinet shop. It's easy to work with carbide-tipped tools and simple to apply. Here's the basic process.

Cut the laminate at least ½ in. oversize in both length and width. Apply contact cement (aerosol cans are convenient) to the back of the laminate and to the mating surface, called the *substrate*. After the cement tacks up (it will lose its sheen and will no longer stick to your finger), place a few dowels across the substrate to hold the sur-faces apart while you position the laminate **(A)**. Place the laminate on the dowels with an even overhang around all four edges of the substrate. Use a roller or bullnose piece of scrap to press a section into place between two of the dowels, tacking the plastic laminate into place **(B)**. Slide the dowels out from in between, pressing the laminate down as you go **(C)**. After pressing the entire piece firmly in place, install a flush-trimming bit in a router, and trim the overhanging edges flush **(D)**. Finish up by filing a slight chamfer on all the edges to ease the sharpness of the plastic **(E)**.

> ⚠ **WARNING If you decide to apply laminate to a wide panel, such as for the panel of a crosscut sled, you should laminate both sides of the piece to help keep it from warping. If you apply laminate to only one side, you will create an imbalance in the way the panel absorbs moisture from the atmosphere. This imbalance will cause the panel to warp severely.**

Blades and Cutters

Installing Blades

➤ Installing a Blade
(p. 68)

➤ Setting Up a Stack
Dado (p. 69)

Cleaning a Blade

➤ Cleaning a Blade
(p. 70)

J UST AS YOU WOULDN'T EXPECT a Ferrari with worn, unbalanced tires to hug the road, you can't expect a hardy, well-designed tablesaw to do great work with a dull or poorly manufactured blade. To cut well, a sawblade must be sharp, and it must run true with minimal wobble, or *runout*. Like a set of tires, a blade is subject to a lot of stresses in use. It must withstand abrasion, friction, and heat as well as terrific centrifugal force.

A blade must also suit the job at hand, whether sawing lumber, plywood, medium-density fiberboard (MDF), plastic laminate, or other materials and whether ripping, crosscutting, sawing joints, or shaping wood. A look at any manufacturer's offering of blades will assure you that there is no short-age of choices. In this section, I demystify the world of blades and other cutters to help you choose those that suit your work and budget.

Blade Anatomy and Terminology

First off, let's get the terms down. The size of a blade is designated by its diameter, measured from tooth tip to tooth tip across the center of the blade. The blade itself consists of a steel plate with the arbor hole at the center. The plate may have expansion slots and/or body slots cut through it. Around its perimeter are the teeth, which do the actual cutting, and scalloped gullets in between. All of these features combine to make a better or worse blade and can help you determine

BLADE SHAPES AND FEATURES

Sawblades come in a wide variety of shapes and with various features. Although all blades have a plate, arbor hole, teeth, and gullets, they may or may not include slots in the plate or anti-kickback shoulders. The four shapes shown here represent typical combination, all-purpose, crosscut, and rip blades.

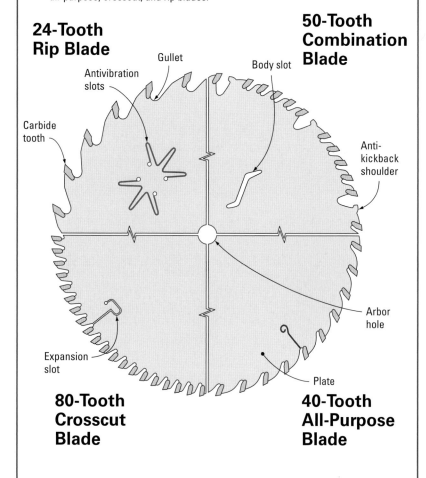

24-Tooth Rip Blade

Gullet

Antivibration slots

Carbide tooth

50-Tooth Combination Blade

Body slot

Anti-kickback shoulder

Arbor hole

Expansion slot

80-Tooth Crosscut Blade

Plate

40-Tooth All-Purpose Blade

the type of cutter most suitable to your work and budget.

Plate and Arbor Hole

The blade's plate, or body, must be flat and stay flat to keep the sawteeth moving in a direct line for a clean cut. Any deviation from a flat plane is called runout, which leads to rough cuts because some teeth sway more to the side as the blade wobbles. Manufacturers of better-quality blades maintain runout tolerances under .003 in. (three thousandths of an inch.)

You can measure the approximate runout at the perimeter of a blade by using a dial indicator, as shown in the photo below. I say *approximate* because any sideways deflection will represent a combination of blade runout and arbor flange runout. If your total runout is less than about .005 on a 10-in.-dia. blade, you're in pretty good shape. Make sure there's no dirt on the arbor flange; and if possible, rotate the blade at the arbor or at the belt to avoid deflecting the blade by hand.

You can measure runout on a blade using a dial indicator. Spin the blade slowly by hand, noting any sideways deflection on the indicator.

▶ See "Assess the Arbor Assembly" on p. 104.

⚠ WARNING **Make sure to unplug the saw when gauging runout.**

The arbor hole should be precisely machined to fit on the saw arbor without slop. Arbor holes are $^5/_8$ in. dia. on 10-in. (and most smaller) blades; 1-in.-dia. arbor holes are common on 12-in. and larger tablesaw blades. An oversize hole can cause a blade to gallop, introducing saw vibration and perhaps compromising the consistency of depth on grooves or other non-through cuts. A blade with a poorly fitting arbor hole may indicate an inferior blade design or simply poor quality control.

Blade Slots

Sawblades can build up considerable heat in use, causing them to expand and perhaps warp if design measures aren't taken to prevent it. Some blades include wide slots in the body that allow air to circulate around the blade, helping keep it cool. They're often found in thin-kerf blades, which are particularly susceptible to warping because their thinner plates have less mass to absorb and dissipate the heat.

Expansion slots allow a hot blade to expand without warping. These laser-cut slots, which take various forms, are spaced around the perimeter of a blade, where the heat tends to build up. Some blades also include antivibration slots to reduce sideways blade flutter.

WHAT ABOUT STEEL BLADES?

Tungsten carbide has been a real boon to the woodworking world. It's so effective and durable as a cutter that blades with steel teeth have pretty much gone the way of the vinyl record and the rotary telephone. Although a carbide blade costs considerably more, you'll get proportionately lots more life from it, and it won't be visiting the sharpening shop nearly as often. But don't throw away your steel blades; they're excellent for sawing up scrap construction lumber that may contain hidden nails and other hardware. (And, of course, they also make quaint wall clocks for the shop.)

Wide slots cut into a blade help cooling air circulate around the blade in use.

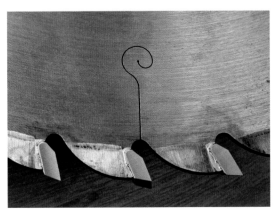

Curlicue-shaped expansion slots that span the perimeter of this blade allow it to accommodate heat expansion without warping.

The antivibration slots cut into this blade are intended to reduce blade flutter.

Teeth and Gullets

Sawteeth take a number of forms, each designed for a particular function. The gullets between the teeth serve as temporary reservoirs for sawdust and chips as the teeth move through the workpiece. The fewer the teeth, the deeper the gullets. The brazing of the carbide teeth to the plate can provide some indication of the quality of work that went into making the blade. Look for clean, consistent joints where the teeth meet the plate. The teeth on premium-quality blades are made from fine-grain C-3 or C-4 carbide particles, which ensure longer life. Inferior teeth made from larger-grain carbide will dull more quickly as the larger particles break away in use. Better blades also exhibit a clean, polished tooth surface.

▶ TOUGH ENOUGH BUT A LITTLE BRITTLE

Carbide teeth are very tough. They'll cut through the hardest of woods and even soft metals like brass and aluminum. However, carbide is brittle and suffers from contact with iron, steel, and other hard metals. Don't use carbide blades if you suspect imbedded nails or other hardware in a board. Teeth not only can crack but can sometimes completely fly off—yet another reason to wear your safety glasses.

Carbide teeth that encounter nails or other hardware can shatter and even break off completely.

The lumpy, inconsistent brazing behind the teeth on the left-hand blade mark its quality as something less than that of the premium-grade blade at the right.

The thickness of a tooth determines the width of the sawcut, called the *kerf*. The saw kerf from a typical 10-in. blade is 1/8 in. (.125 in.), although most *thin-kerf* blades make a cut approximately 3/32 in. wide. Teeth are shaped (or ground) to serve particular purposes. The most common tooth types are *flat-top grind* (FTG), *alternate-top bevel* (ATB), and *triple-chip grind* (TCG). Variations include high-ATB teeth and combination blades, which have teeth with a mix of ATB and FTG grinds.

- **Flat-top grind** teeth have no bevel and rip into wood like a chisel chopping a mortise. They remove wood quickly but not very cleanly, tending to cut roughly on the side of a kerf. They are meant for ripping wood, and will cause considerable tearout on crosscuts. FTG teeth are also called *raker* teeth and create a flat-bottomed groove.

- **Alternate-top bevel** teeth are ground at opposing angles. The bevel angle may be low or high; steep angles are designated by some manufacturers as high-ATB (HATB). The bevel creates a point that shears cleanly through wood fibers at the edge of the saw kerf, reducing tearout, particularly when crosscutting. The steeper the angle, the cleaner the cut but the quicker the point dulls. Most modern all-purpose blades consist of an ATB tooth configuration. These teeth create a V-bottomed groove.

TOOTH TYPES

Flat-Top Grind (FTG)

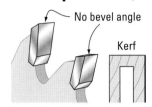

No bevel angle

Kerf

Alternate-Top Bevel (ATB)

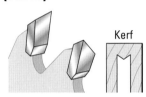

Kerf

Combination

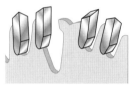

Kerf

FTG interspersed with ATB teeth

Triple-Chip Grind (TCG)

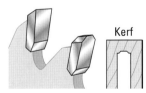

Kerf

FTG teeth alternate with chamfered teeth.

► BEVEL AND RAKE ANGLES

The geometry of a tooth includes two crucial angles that largely determine the way a tooth cuts. The *bevel angle* is the angle across the top edge of the tooth. The *rake angle*, or *hook,* is the angle of the tooth face relative to a line drawn through the blade's center.

The degree of bevel angle determines a tooth's durability and shearing action. The steeper the bevel, the cleaner the cut but the quicker the point wears down. A positive rake angle allows a more aggressive cut but with some exit tearout, depending on the blade quality. A blade with zero or negative rake reduces tearout and inhibits the tendency of a blade to self-feed, making it a good choice for radial-arm and sliding compound-miter saws.

Bevel Angles

FTG
0° bevel
Fast ripping, rough crosscutting

ATB
10 to 20°, typ.
General-purpose ripping and crosscutting

High-ATB
25 to 38°, typ.
Tearout-free crosscutting, especially in plywood

Hook Angles

0 to 20°, typ.
Positive rake
Line through center of blade
Allows fast feeding, possible exit tearout

Zero rake
Reduces climbing on overhead saws; minimal exit tearout.

0 to 6°, typ.
Negative rake
No climbing, with minimal tearout; requires stronger feeding on tablesaw.

- **Combination** teeth typically consist of groups of four ATB teeth preceded by a raker tooth, with each group separated by deep gullets. The design intent is to allow good ripping capabilities (aided by the raker teeth), while also providing clean crosscuts from the ATB teeth. This once-common combination tooth design has largely been superseded by the ATB configuration. Because the raker teeth sit a bit below the ATB tooth points, these teeth create a kerf bottom that's something between a V-groove and a flat groove.

- **Triple-chip grind** teeth consist of alternating FTG teeth and trapezoidal-shaped chamfered teeth. The chamfered teeth rough out the kerf, while the FTG teeth rake the cut clean. This combination of teeth effectively nibbles away at dense materials like MDF and plastic laminate but maintains good blade life since there are no beveled teeth tips to wear down quickly. Because the chamfered teeth project a bit beyond the FTG teeth, these teeth do not create a flat-bottomed groove.

The number of teeth on a blade depends to some degree on the diameter of the blade. For example, a 10-in. general-purpose blade typically has 40 teeth, whereas a 12-in. blade designed for the same purpose might have 48 teeth. A 10-in. crosscut blade usually has 80 teeth, and a 12-in. crosscut blade may have 96 teeth. However, these numbers can vary because there certainly don't seem to be many ironclad design rules in the world of tablesaw blades.

Some *anti-kickback* blades include high shoulders that intrude into the gullets behind some of the teeth. These shoulders

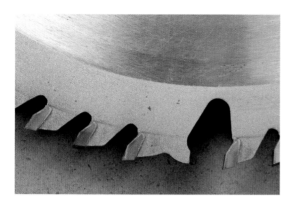

The high shoulder behind this group of teeth limits the amount of wood the blade can bite into at a time, forcing slower feed speeds to reduce the chance of kickback.

limit the depth of cut, preventing overfeeding, which can cause kickback, especially if a splitter isn't used. That said—you really should get in the habit of using your splitter.

The Right Blade for the Job

Sawblade design is a fairly complex art. There seem to be as many types of blades as there are women's shoe styles. (Well, okay, that's stretching it.) But take heart; by following a few guidelines, you can cut through the clutter of blade choices to ferret out the ones you need.

To some degree, a blade can be defined by its intended purpose. Taking that approach, we can divide the types into the rough categories of *rip blades*, *crosscut blades*, and *all-purpose blades*. In addition, I'll discuss blades designed to saw dense materials like plastic laminate and solid-surface materials like Corian®.

Note: To simplify explanation here, the number of teeth discussed in the following sections refer to 10-in. blades. Larger blades will have proportionately more teeth.

► THE BOTTOM LINE ON SAWBLADES

Don't be daunted by the enormous variety of sawblade choices or worry that you'll have to skimp on groceries to afford all the ones you'll need. Truth is, you can get by with a single premium-quality all-purpose blade, which may set you back somewhere around a hundred bucks.

The drawback to having only one blade is that it may not rip as quickly through thick hardwoods, and it may require more frequent sharpenings if you're sawing plastic laminates and other dense materials. When the blade's at the sharpener's, you'll have downtime. Aside from that, a premium-quality general-purpose blade should provide good to excellent rips and crosscuts in solid wood and all sorts of sheet goods. On the other hand, the more skilled you get at the tablesaw, the more you'll want to add special-purpose blades to your collection.

A 24-tooth rip blade (left), an 80-tooth crosscut blade (center), and a 40-tooth all-purpose blade can tackle the brunt of work in many small shops.

The Right Blade for the Job

Stated tooth count applies to 10-in. blades.

JOB	BLADE CHOICES	COMMENTS
Ripping solid wood	24-tooth FTG	This "rip" blade cuts fast but coarse; good for initial rough sizing of pieces
	40-tooth or 50-tooth ATB or combination blade	Rips slower but cleaner; premium-quality blades require little or no cleanup
Crosscutting solid wood and general plywood sawing	40-tooth to 80-tooth ATB or combination blade	Blades with more teeth generally cut cleaner, but a premium 40-tooth blade may cut better than a mediocre 80-tooth blade
Sawing MDF, Melamine, and particleboard	40-tooth to 80-tooth ATB or TCG	ATB blades tend to cut cleaner but dull faster than TCG blades
Sawing plastic laminate, nonferrous metal, and plastics	80-tooth TCG	ATB blades can be used instead but may blunt quickly in these dense materials
Joinery	40-tooth or 50-tooth ATB	A premium-quality blade will create glue-ready long- and cross-grain joints

FTC, flat-top grind; *ATB*, alternate-top bevel; *TCG*, triple-chip grind.

► THIN-KERF BLADES

If your saw's motor is less than 2-hp, you may experience bogging down when ripping thick hardwoods. If so, consider getting a thin-kerf blade. The teeth on these blades are typically about 3/32 in. wide. Because they remove less wood than a standard kerf blade, less force is required to make the cut. The downside? Because the blade plate is thinner, it's more subject to fluttering, or runout, which produces a rougher cut than one made with a thicker-bodied blade.

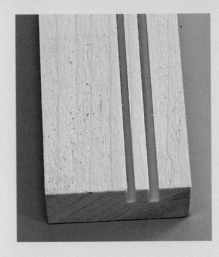

The 3/32-in.-wide teeth on a thin-kerf blade make a kerf that's only three quarters the size of the standard kerf (at right), allowing the thin teeth to chew through wood a lot easier.

Rip Blades

Ripping solid wood (sawing parallel to the grain) is best done with a blade that has about 24 FTG teeth and a positive rake of about 20 degrees. Such a blade will rip quickly, although it won't leave a very clean surface. If you're using it to rip to final width, allow a bit of extra width to joint away afterward.

Don't expect to get a clean cut in plywood or other sheet goods with a rip blade. I primarily use this kind of blade to saw lumber into rough-size cabinet and furniture parts. It will do the job quickly and saves wear and tear on my premium all-purpose blade. Because I don't need a rip blade to produce a flawless cut, I don't pay top dollar for it. Mine cost about $50.

► See "Dressing Stock" on p. 201.

Crosscut Blades

A 60-tooth or 80-tooth ATB crosscut blade produces a clean edge when sawing stock to length or when making miters. A premium-quality blade will produce little or no exit tearout. High-angle ATB teeth will ensure the cleanest of cutting, even when sawing plywood, Melamine®-coated particleboard (MCP), or other sheet goods with delicate facings. A moderately low rake angle of about 10 degrees allows easy feeding and good cutting on a tablesaw. A blade with zero or negative rake is a good choice for radial-arm saws and sliding compound-miter saws because it prevents climbing.

Truth is, I seldom use a crosscut blade on my tablesaw because my premium all-purpose blade makes comparable crosscuts.

► GAUGING CUT QUALITY

The kind of surface you can expect from a premium-grade all-purpose blade depends on the tooth shape and the overall manufacturing tolerances. Top-quality ATB blades can leave a smooth surface with virtually no tooth scoring, as seen on the bottom sample in the photo, which was made with a $110 blade. A surface this smooth is ready for gluing. To serve as an exposed edge on a project, it would need only a light sanding or handplaning. A blade that cuts this well on a long-grain edge should also leave little or no cross-grain tearout.

Good-quality blades may create some light scoring like that on the center sample, which was made from a decent, but not premium, quality blade that cost about $75. This surface is fine for gluing in most circumstances but would need jointing and sanding to serve as an acceptable exposed edge. The surface on the top sample, which was made from a $50 FTG rip blade, is fine, considering that the blade is intended for quick, rough ripping.

These sample cuts were made from a premium-quality 40-tooth blade (bottom), a medium-quality 40-tooth blade (center), and a 24-tooth rip blade (top).

If you don't already own a premium-quality all-purpose blade, I would recommend checking one out first, as you may well be happy with the crosscuts it makes. If you do decide to buy a premium crosscut blade, expect to pay between $80 and $120.

All-Purpose Blades

The 40-tooth or 50-tooth ATB blades with a 15-degree to 20-degree positive hook are the real workhorses of many shops, where they live on the saw 90 percent of the time. They're sometimes called "combination blades," although that technical designation is often reserved for blades with a combination of ATB and FTG teeth. All-purpose blades are designed to serve a rip/crosscut compromise. They'll rip cleanly and fairly quickly, but not as fast as a rip blade with FTG teeth. The ATB teeth make nice crosscuts too, although maybe not as nice as a crosscut blade with more teeth, depending

▶ See "Teeth and Gullets" p. 54.

on the quality of the blades.

The key word here is *quality*. There are lots and lots of all-purpose, combination blades on the market, but this is not the time to surrender to your frugal nature. This is a blade you'll use a lot! A cheap one will make you sorry, and a top-shelf version will make you a better woodworker. Expect to pay $80 to $110 for the real thing. What brand, you ask? Look to woodworking magazines, which regularly run comparison tests, or visit online woodworking message boards for good suggestions.

Blades for Dense Materials

If you're a well-rounded woodworker, you'll probably find yourself working occasionally with dense materials like MDF, MCP, and plastic laminate (one brand is Formica). You might even have occasion to cut up some solid-surface material like Corian. When it comes to this kind of brutal stuff, you might want to spare the pointy teeth on your expensive ATB blades.

This would be the time to pull out a blade with TCG teeth. The combination of chamfered and FTG teeth can withstand the blows to the material better than ATB teeth can and still leave a clean edge. You can spend about $40 for a 40-tooth TCG blade or up to $80 or more for an 80-tooth version. Unless you work with a lot of dense material, it's probably safe to steer to a mid-range price here.

▶ See "Teeth and Gullets" p. 54.

Dado Heads

Dado heads provide a quick way to cut rabbets, dadoes, grooves, tenons, and half-lap joints on the tablesaw. There are two common forms of dado head: a *wobble dado* and a *stack dado*. A wobble dado is simply a blade that's mounted on an angled hub that causes the blade to tilt back and forth as it spins, cutting a wide swath in the workpiece. A stack dado consists of two outer blades with a selection of cutters in between, called chippers. By mounting the appropriate number of chippers and shims between the blades, you can create a dado of the desired width.

A dado head is invaluable for cutting rabbets, dadoes, grooves, tenons, and open mortises on the tablesaw.

As with regular sawblades, dado heads are available with steel or carbide teeth. Carbide costs more but stays sharp much longer than steel. This is important because dull teeth will tear wood fibers and lead to rough cuts. For strong, neat-looking joinery, your dadoes and rabbets need to have clean, squarely cut sides and straight, flat bottoms. Of course, this kind of quality doesn't come at a discount. However, once you pony up the money for a premium dado head, it's unlikely you'll ever have to buy another unless you cut dadoes all day long, day after day.

Wobble Dado

At $50 or more, a wobble dado head is a relatively inexpensive tool. Wobble dadoes come in a variety of forms, depending on the manufacturer. All of the configurations cause the blade (or two blades) to spin at

▶ BLADE STABILIZERS

Blade stabilizers, also called *stiffeners* or *dampeners*, are precisely machined metal disks intended to reduce blade vibration, producing cleaner cuts. You can install a single stabilizer on the outer face of a blade or use two, sandwiching a blade between. However, keep in mind that an "inner" stabilizer mounted against the arbor flange shifts the blade's position in relationship to your rip fence scale, your throat plate slot, and any jig that runs in the table slots.

Some argue that stabilizers help if you have a shaky saw that's transmitting vibration to the blade or if you're working with a cheap or thin-kerf blade. Others consider them a gimmick. In my experience, they're of little help. If your saw is well tuned and outfitted with a premium blade, it's unlikely you'll notice any difference in cut quality. Although stabilizers cost only $15 or $20, I feel that the money would be better spent toward a premium blade or perhaps a link belt to reduce saw vibration.

▶ See "Stabilize the Saw and Minimize Vibration" on p. 108.

A stabilizer is a thick metal disk that mounts directly against the blade body.

A wobble dado consists of a blade sandwiched between two angled hubs that cause the whipping blade to cut a wide swath through the wood.

To adjust the amount of angle on a wobble dado, the hubs are rotated to create the desired width of cut.

A cut from a wobble dado (at left) will require considerable sanding compared to a cut from a good-quality stack dado (at right).

an angle, plowing a dado or groove in the wood. To adjust the amount of angle, you rotate the hubs for the desired width of cut. What you're actually doing is introducing an enormous amount of runout in the blade to make a wide cut. Unfortunately, the geometry of the cut yields an angle of attack that tends to create tearout at the edges of the cut as well as a bottom that's not truly flat. Wobble dadoes can also be a bit fussy to adjust because tightening the arbor nut can change the width setting. It usually takes several test cuts and readjustments to get the desired setting.

Undeniably, the tool works, but it's definitely a shortcut that may not be worth the cost savings if you're cutting dadoes for cabinetry and furniture work. You'll spend considerable time sanding and puttying to deal with the tearout, especially if you work with plywood and other sheet goods. Wider

dadoes may also show a gap at the bottom where the mating member butts in, due to the arc-like path the teeth on a wobble dado follow. My advice is to skip buying a wobble dado and save up for a good-quality stack dado. The hundred or so bucks that you would save will end up costing you lots in terms of time and compromised work.

Stack Dado

The most common type of dado head is a stack dado, consisting of two outer blades with a number of chippers sandwiched in between, each having two, three, or four teeth. The outer blades cleanly slice the dado walls while the chippers plow out the waste in between. When necessary to fine-tune the width of a dado head, paper, plastic, or metal shims can be placed between the components to widen the intended cut by as little as a few thousandths of an inch. For

A stack dado consists of an inner and an outer sawblade between which are sandwiched chippers of various thicknesses and shims for fine-tuning the width of cut.

If it's necessary to compact a stack dado enough to accommodate undersize hardwood plywood, have a machine shop grind away about .020 in. from each side of a ¼-in. chipper.

example, on my stack dado a $^1/_4$-in. chipper, a $^1/_8$-in. chipper, and a $^1/_{16}$-in. chipper plus a few appropriate shims will create a $^{25}/_{32}$-in. cut, which is perfect for typical "$^3/_4$-in." hardwood plywood.

A stack dado will typically cut a dado or groove from $^1/_4$ in. to $^{13}/_{16}$ in. wide, with the $^1/_4$-in.-wide groove being made with just the two outer blades. Some sets include a $^3/_{32}$-in.-wide chipper, allowing you to make a perfectly sized cut in hardwood plywood, which is nominally undersize by about $^1/_{32}$ in. If you find that your dado head won't stack to accommodate undersize hardwood plywood, it's not a big deal to have a machine shop grind down the center of a chipper to create a thinner cut, as shown in the photo at above.

Stack dadoes are usually available in either a 6-in. or an 8-in. diameter. Most rabbets and dadoes are shallow enough that a

6-in.-dia. model will serve just fine. However, if you like to cut bridle joints to make frames and other assemblies, you'll appreciate the depth of cut that an 8-in. dado head offers. Expect to pay between $100 and $300 for a good carbide-tipped stack dado.

See "Bridle Joint" on p. 198.

[TIP] For efficiency when setting up a stack dado, maintain a list of the combinations of chippers and shims that yield common cut widths.

Specialty Blades

There are any number of custom-ground blades and other cutters designed for specific purposes. For example, Forrest Manufacturing offers an ATB blade with half-flat tips for cutting perfectly flat-bottomed $^1/_8$-in.-wide grooves for sawing spline slots or narrow finger joints. Ridge Carbide makes a blade with $^7/_{32}$-in.-wide teeth for cutting snug-fitting drawer side grooves for hardwood plywood in one pass. You'll find many other choices in blade manufacturers' catalogs and on their websites. In addition, many companies offer molding heads and other specialty cutters.

▶ FREUD'S DIAL-A-WIDTH DADO SET

Like a regular stack dado, the Dial-A-Width Dado Set by Freud® consists of two outer blades and a selection of chippers to be placed between them. However, this cleverly designed dado head allows you to fine-tune the width of cut by simply rotating a hub on the outer blade, eliminating the need for shimming. This can be a real time-saver if you do a lot of dado joinery.

The Freud Dial-A-Width Dado Set consists of two outer blades and several internal chippers, just like a standard stack dado. However, the width of the cut can be adjusted by turning a hub on the outer blade, driving a threaded section of the hub inward or outward against the inner chipper to slightly change the blade's spacing.

FORREST #1 CUSTOM GRIND

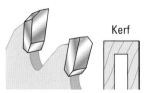

Kerf

Half of ATB tooth ground flat for square-bottom kerf

Molding Heads

A tablesaw molding head can be used to create moldings for trim, picture frames, and other decorative work. It can even create tongue-and-groove joints and locking miters, among other joinery chores. Sears® and Delta® both offer molding heads, although the Delta model seems difficult to track down these days. The Sears Craftsman® molding head kit costs about $100 and comes with eight different knife sets. A total of about 30 different knife styles are available for it, although only as steel cutters. They'll do a decent job but can't be

This blade from Ridge Carbide will cut a 7/32-in. groove in one pass, perfect for fitting undersize 1/4-in. hardwood plywood.

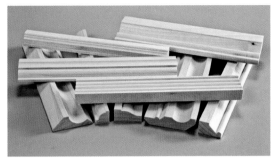

A tablesaw molding head can produce an amazing variety of moldings for use in furniture making and architectural woodwork like room trim.

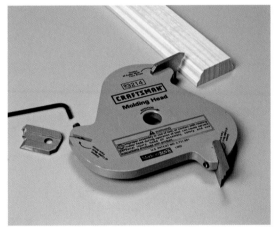

The Craftsman molding head can be outfitted with a variety of steel knives, which lock solidly in place with a setscrew that runs through a hole in the knife.

The carbide cutter "plugs" on the innovative Magic Molder rotate into place on a registration pin and lock down with hefty setscrews.

expected to stay sharp forever, especially if you're shaping a lot of hardwood. And cutting MDF or other composite material will dull them quickly.

LRH Enterprises offers a premium molding head for those who want to do more extensive molding on the tablesaw. Called the Magic Molder, this molding head is designed for safety and accepts a very wide variety of carbide knives, which will hold up well even when cutting hardwoods or MDF. It's a very well balanced, carefully manufactured tool with chip-limiting capabilities for safer feeding. A basic starter kit with the head and two different knife sets will cost you about $300, with additional knife sets running about $100 each.

►STAYING SHARP

So how do you know when to sharpen a blade? Pay attention to the way it cuts and the way it looks under strong magnification. If a blade starts to smoke, create excessive tearout, or require more feed pressure, it may be getting dull. Try cleaning it first to see if that helps. Look at the tooth tips under a 10× loupe; if they're starting to round over, they may need sharpening. The best reference is to take a few sample cuts when the blade is new or freshly resharpened. Rip some bland maple or pine, and crosscut some plywood. (Oak veneer plywood is best because of its tendency to tear out.) Mark the samples with the blade name and stash them for future comparison.

It's often best to send the blade back to the manufacturer for sharpening because service personnel know exactly how to handle the particular grinds of their blades. Alternatively, you might try calling a local professional woodshop to get a recommendation for a good sharpener.

The pitch that's beginning to build up on these teeth will eventually cause the blade to heat up, scorching the wood during a cut.

If you'd like to make moldings and don't have a shaper or good router table, a molding head may be a good choice for you. For occasional work of this sort, the Craftsman model provides better economy, as long as it includes the types of knives you want. For better quality and safety when producing larger molding runs, consider the Magic Molder. Also note that a molding head allows you to cut profiles in the center of a wide board—a place that is out of the reach of both routers and shapers.

►For more on molding heads, see p. 205.

Blade Maintenance and Storage

If there's one thing that most woodworkers are guilty of, it's working with dirty sawblades. A blade that's gummed up with baked-on pitch and crud can cause burning on cuts, especially on blades with minimal side clearance. Dirty blades also heat up more, which can shorten the life of the teeth. Fortunately, it's dead simple to clean even a badly gummed up blade. It takes about 5 minutes using commonly available, environmentally friendly cleaning products. Make sure to coat the blades with rust protectant afterward.

The built-up, burned-on gum and pitch on these teeth comes off easily with concentrated citrus cleaner and a brass bristle brush.

▶ See "Cleaning a Blade" on p. 70

[TIP] Do not use oven cleaner on blades. According to some blade manufacturers, it breaks down the cobalt binder that cements the carbide particles together.

Keep your blades sharp. A good-quality carbide blade will stay sharp a long time. Unless you're doing production work with it, a blade may need sharpening only once every 2 years or 3 years. Equally important, protect the brittle teeth from hard knocks. Don't lay blades on your saw table and never stack them directly on top of each other; at least sandwich them between cardboard. I store my blades in a dedicated cabinet to keep them safe and organized.

This blade cabinet includes slide-out shelves made from pegboard, which allows the desiccant packages in the bottom section to absorb moisture throughout the cabinet.

A

B

C

D

E

VARIATION

Installing a Blade

⚠ **WARNING** Always unplug the saw before changing the blade!

Slide a blade onto the saw arbor **(A)**, then press on opposite sides of the arbor hole to make sure the blade is seated firmly against the arbor flange. Install the plate washer against the blade in the same manner **(B)**. Next, the nut goes on. Left-tilt saws have a standard arbor thread (tightening clockwise), whereas right-tilt saws have a reverse thread. To insert the nut into the narrow throat plate opening, I grasp it between my index and middle fingers **(C)**, and then press it against the end of the arbor **(D)**. Still using the same two fingers, I rotate the nut just enough to get it started on the thread. Then it's a simple matter of quickly spinning it all the rest of the way on and tightening it with my saw wrenches **(E)**. Don't overdo it, though. Keep in mind that the blade rotation actually tightens the nut in use. If you apply too much wrench torque, you can eventually flatten the outer blade washer.

[VARIATION] If your saw doesn't allow for use of two wrenches, don't lodge a piece of wood against the teeth to hold the blade. You can bend a tooth that way. Instead, use a rag or gloved hand to hold the blade while you tighten the arbor nut.

Setting Up a Stack Dado

Setting up a stack dado is a simple matter of mounting the two blades with the appropriate size and number of chippers and shims between them to create the desired width of cut. For easy adjustment of the cut width after the initial setup, it's best to install the shims between the outermost chippers and blade.

Mount the first blade, making sure that the teeth "lean" toward the outside of the cut **(A)**. Mount the first chipper, making sure that the chipper plate doesn't rest against the blade teeth and that the blade teeth and chipper teeth aren't touching **(B)**. Mount the next chipper, spacing its teeth relatively evenly between the teeth of the preceding chipper.

If the setup requires a few shims, insert one or two of them next **(C)**. Install the final chipper and any remaining shims **(D)**. Finally, mount the outer blade, installing the flange washer backward if there isn't enough arbor length to mount it in it's usual orientation **(E)**. Attach the nut, tightening it securely without overdoing the torque. Double-check to make sure that none of the teeth has spun against another during installation.

Take a test-cut in a piece of scrap, then make any necessary adjustments by adding or removing shims. When you arrive at the desired width of cut, it's wise to make a note of the combination of chippers and shims for future reference.

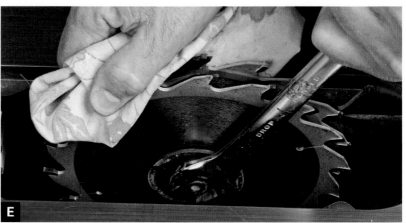

A

B

Cleaning a Blade

I've found that the perfect tray for cleaning blades is a 12-in. pizza pan, but you could lay a blade on a piece of scrap plywood or a stack of newspaper instead. Some woodworkers recommend using mineral spirits, lacquer thinner, or other strong solvents to clean the gum and pitch from a blade, but there's no need to use toxic chemicals. Of all the cleaners I've tried over the years, I've gotten the quickest, best results from environmentally friendly cleaners like the concentrated citrus cleaner and degreaser sold at home supply stores. I've also had excellent success with Simple Green® concentrated cleaner.

Spray a light coating of cleaner on the sawteeth **(A)**. Let it sit for just a few minutes, then lightly scrub the teeth with a brass bristle brush **(B)**. You'll find it takes very little effort to remove even hardened gunk this way. After cleaning both sides of the blade, rinse it well with warm water to remove the cleaner and gunk residue. Dry the blade well, then spray it with a metal protectant to prevent rust **(C)**. There are plenty of products on the market for this purpose, and WD-40® works fine too. Spread the protectant all over the blade, then wipe off the excess with a clean, soft rag or paper towel **(D)**.

C

D

Splitters and Guards

Splitters

➤ Making a Wooden Splitter (p. 81)

➤ Making an Aluminum Splitter (p. 84)

Kickback

➤ Kickback in Action (p. 82)

I T'S NO SECRET THAT A TABLESAW isn't the safest tool in a shop. Some sources report 30,000 tablesaw-related visits to U.S. emergency rooms every year. Others claim it's as high as 60,000. Let's just say it's a lot. So we need to be careful. The dangers that lurk at a tablesaw are specific and can be protected against.

In essence, there are two ways you can be harmed by a tablesaw. The first is getting cut by the blade. The second is getting smacked by a flying piece of stock. If you're particularly unlucky, both can happen at the same time. Although you might suspect that most accidents involve blade and skin, the truth is that the majority of injuries are caused by wood being "kicked back" by the saw. In this section, I'll discuss how to keep danger at bay when working at the tablesaw.

First, we'll take a look at defeating kickback by using a splitter or riving knife, then we'll see about guarding our digits from those sawteeth.

What Causes Kickback?

When working at the tablesaw, there are two ways that a piece of wood can be thrown back at you. One is when a ripping—typically a narrow strip—ejects rearward like an arrow from between the blade and the fence. This can happen if your push stick heel slips from the stock. To avoid injury, never stand directly behind a board being ripped.

True kickback is when a workpiece is thrown upward and backward at fierce speed toward you. This has probably happened to anyone who has worked at a tablesaw for

▶ QUICK-CHANGE TRADITIONAL GUARDS

Some manufacturers have taken steps to ease the removal and replacement of traditional-style blade guards, making the operation tool-free and relatively quick. For example, the splitter/guard on the Steel City Toolworks hybrid saw simply slips into a spring-loaded mount cover under the throat plate, while the rear of the unit mounts and dismounts with a few turns of a knob at the rear of the saw. Other manufacturers have taken different approaches to the same problem.

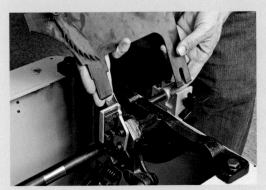

This quick-change guard slips into a bracket under the throat plate and under a locking knob at the rear of the saw.

Biesemeyer's snap-in spreader.

Note: Bracket-mounted aftermarket splitters aren't designed for portable saws—only contractors' saws and cabinet saws.

Bracket-Mounted Splitters

There is a small variety of commercial splitters on the market. All of them mount and dismount easily and quickly enough that you'll actually use them. Here's a brief view of the current playing field.

Biesemeyer's snap-in spreader is very convenient to use. It takes about 2 seconds to install and 5 seconds to remove. It simply snaps into its bracket, which is mounted inside the saw. To remove the splitter, remove the throat plate, retract a spring-loaded knob, and lift it out.

The nearly $1/8$-in.-thick splitter is rock solid and will withstand an accidental blow from a board without bending. Its thickness, however, prevents use with thin-kerf blades, so this might not be the best choice for an underpowered saw. Models are available for all left- and right-tilt Delta cabinet and contractor's saws, as well as for certain Jet®, Powermatic®, and General® models. The unit is pricey and can sell for as much as $190, although a web search turned up several discount dealers offering some versions for as little as $125.

[TIP] **Initial mounting and alignment of an aftermarket splitter can be fussy and time-consuming, but you'll have to do it only once, so take the time to do it right.**

Delta's removable splitter is a lighter-duty, slightly less convenient version of the Biesemeyer splitter. The metal is thinner and less substantial, but the splitter can be used with thin-kerf blades. It's attached and removed by loosening and tightening a knob on the mounting bracket.

This takes a few moments longer than does the Biesemeyer, but the unit costs considerably less, at about $30. Unfortunately, it fits only Delta saws.

Delta's disappearing splitter simply pushes down below the saw table when not in use, so it never has to be removed from the saw. It is thin and prone to bending but can be used with thin-kerf blades. Its convenience is its best attribute because at about $140, it's not cheap and will fit only a right-tilting Unisaw.

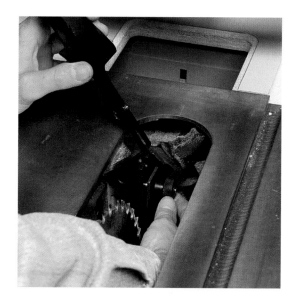

Delta's removable splitter.

MISSING: PAUL'S PAWLS

You may notice in various photos in this book that the spring-loaded barbed pawls are missing from my Unisaw's Biesemeyer splitter. That's because I've found that splitter pawls are more aggravation than they're worth. They impede push stick travel on very narrow rip cuts and can trap narrow pieces between the pawl and the splitter. European woodworkers must not think too highly of them either, as you don't see pawls on Euro-style riving knives. Anyway, this is just by way of explanation.

I'm certainly not recommending that you remove your pawls.

Delta's disappearing splitter.

Excalibur's Merlin splitter.

Excalibur's Merlin splitter somewhat resembles a traditional splitter but without the blade cover. It's a long, tall piece of thin metal that connects to two brackets: one under the throat plate and one at the rear of the saw. It will work with thin-kerf blades

and detaches quickly without tools. (A dowel can be slipped through a hole in the installed throat plate to depress the release.) Because of its size, it can be a bit intrusive for some operations. For example, when ripping narrow pieces, you'll need a tall push stick. It costs about $100 and will fit lots of different saw models.

Throat Plate–Mounted Splitters

There are quite a few ways to mount a splitter in a shopmade throat plate, also called a zero-clearance insert (ZCI). As shown earlier, a ZCI is easy to make and improves cut quality while preventing small pieces from jamming in an oversize throat opening. A ZCI offers a mounting platform for a splitter, whether commercial or shopmade.

One commercial model is made by Micro Jig. The MJ splitter installs into holes that you make in your ZCI using the drilling jig supplied with the splitter. A variety of these inexpensive MJ splitters are available to suit different blade widths and working circumstances.

▶ For more on zero-clearance inserts, see Section 2.

▶ For buying information, see "Resources" on p. 217.

You can also make your own ZCI splitters from wood or aluminum angle. The easiest approach is to simply glue a splitter into the ZCI at the far end of the blade slot. This has the benefit of minimizing the distance between the blade and the splitter and can be used for ripping stock up to 1 in. or so thick.

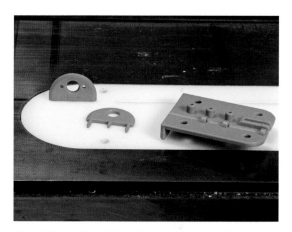

The Micro Jig MJ splitter installs in holes you drill in a zero-clearance insert plate using the supplied drilling jig.

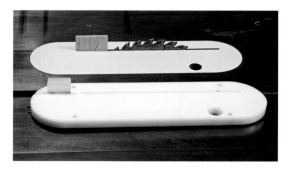

Splitters can be made from wood glued into a throat plate slot or from aluminum angle screwed to the underside of the plate.

Raising the blade much higher will cut away too much of the splitter for it to be effective. For ripping thick stock, install a splitter into an "aft slot" cut behind the main slot.

Aluminum angle (available at hardware stores) provides an easy way to add a strong,

► See "Making a Wooden Splitter" on p. 81.

► See "Making an Aluminum Splitter" on p. 84

► TRADITIONAL SPLITTERS JOIN THE DINOSAURS

Good news for your fingers: Legislation in the United States requires that all new-model tablesaws (manufactured as of 2008) must be equipped with a riving knife that rises, falls, and tilts with the blade. Current models with traditional splitters can be sold on the U.S. market until 2012. After that, *all* tablesaws sold in the country must have a riving knife. There will no longer be any reason to remove and discard a stock splitter because it's too much trouble to remount.

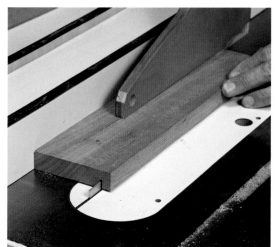

A low-profile splitter can be used for shallow grooves and other non-through cuts.

adjustable splitter to an insert plate. Using smaller angle creates a low-profile splitter that can even be used for shallow grooves and other non-through cuts.

Riving Knives

A riving knife serves the same purpose as a splitter, but much more conveniently. Like a splitter, a riving knife prevents the blade's rising rear teeth from lifting a workpiece and

A riving knife mounts to the blade lifting mechanism and rises, falls, and tilts in alignment with the blade. It can be removed or adjusted up and down to accommodate different diameter blades, and some include an easily detachable blade cover.

kicking it back toward the operator. The difference between a splitter and a riving knife is that the latter rises, falls, and tilts with the blade, allowing the knife to closely hug the curve of the blade, minimizing the danger zone between the rear teeth and the knife.

A true riving knife can be set just below the height of the blade, which means it won't have be removed to saw grooves, joint shoulders, and make other non-through cuts. The reason I stipulate a *true* riving knife is that the riving knife on some recent model saws rises and falls with the blade but won't adjust below it—something to keep in mind when comparing saw features. Many newer model saws come with two riving knives: one that offers attachment for a blade cover, and the other that can sit below the top of the blade for non-through cuts.

Aftermarket Blade Guards

So we've discussed how to beat kickback using a splitter or riving knife. But what's the best way to protect our fingers from that spinning blade? The blade covers on traditional guards offer protection, but they can be pretty cumbersome. Aftermarket overhead guards are a better bet because they're easier to use.

There is a half-dozen or so commercial "overarm" blade guards to choose from. The blade cover typically mounts to a set of pivoting arms that allow the cover to raise and lower easily over the blade. The arms attach to an extending overhead boom that allows you to slide the cover section off to the side or remove the boom entirely to accommodate large, tall workpieces.

Although these blade guards don't offer protection against kickback, they will protect your hands from wandering into the blade. They also keep dust and splinters from flying up into your face. Some offer dust-

▶ SAW STOP: A NEW APPROACH TO TABLESAW SAFETY

When it comes to safety, it's hard to top the Saw Stop tablesaw. In addition to a riving knife to prevent kickback, the machine incorporates an ingenious blade brake that halts a spinning blade instantly upon contact with skin. When the saw's electronic sensor detects flesh, an aluminum block "cartridge" in the cabinet springs against the blade, stopping it within 5 milliseconds and leaving only a slight nick in a hot dog used for demonstration purposes. The action also causes the blade to drop below the saw table in a flash. It's a remarkable thing to watch. Unfortunately, the contact ruins both the brake cartridge (about $80) and the blade, which must be replaced. Still, that hurts a lot less than a hospital bill and a maimed hand.

When the brake detects skin contact, it springs up against the spinning blade, stopping it in an instant, and driving it below the table.

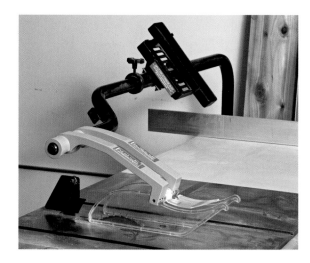 

An overhead blade guard, like this Delta Deluxe model, protects your hands from the blade and prevents upward flying dust and chips. The boom is easily removable when necessary.

An overhead guard won't impede the use of a miter gauge if the fence is adjusted to the left of the guard.

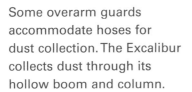

Some overarm guards accommodate hoses for dust collection. The Excalibur collects dust through its hollow boom and column.

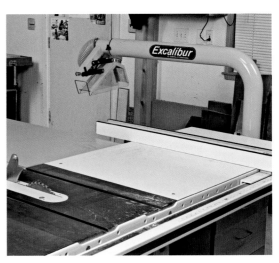

Some overarm guards swing out of the way and/or can be removed entirely to provide clearance when working with large, tall workpieces.

collection capabilities, either by providing a dust port on the blade cover or by using the mounting boom and post as a dust chute.

[TIP] For product reviews and user opinions of aftermarket splitters and guards, consult the web using specific search terms such as "Excalibur overarm guard review."

Although an overarm guard offers side-to-side adjustability, it still impedes ripping of very narrow pieces and interferes with the use of many jigs. All the same, it provides convenient protection for your hands and face (and lungs, with dust collection) while you rip boards and panels and crosscut with a miter gauge. (The fences on most crosscut sleds conflict with the guard.) When shopping for an aftermarket blade guard, here are a few things to consider:

- **Mounting compatibility.** The post typically mounts to either the rear or the end of a side extension table. Some won't work with fence systems that require a rear rail.

- **Ease of use.** Look for a boom that extends without struggle and a blade cover that adjusts up and down easily and that stays parallel to the saw table.

- **Work area clearance.** When working with tall jigs or workpieces, you'll need to get the guard out of the way. On some models, the boom slides far to the right or swings out of the way entirely.

- **Splitter teamwork.** Make sure that the blade cover clears your splitter, allowing unimpeded side-to-side cover adjustment.

- **Dust collection.** I find dust collection capability to be one of the most attractive features of an overarm guard. Not all guards offer a dust port, and with some, it's optional.

Making a Wooden Splitter

It's easy to make a wooden splitter and install it into a zero-clearance throat plate **(A)**. Because the splitter is glued in place, the throat plate material needs to be made of wood or a wood product like MDF. First make the zero-clearance insert plate. (Don't use an old throat plate whose slot may have been widened over time.)

▶ See "Making a Zero-Clearance Throat Plate" on p. 38.

Slot the plate, then saw a splitter from the end of a piece of hardwood scrap to fit the width of the slot exactly **(B)**. You can make the splitter whatever height you like. A projection of 1 in. or so from the plate is fine for general work. Cut the piece to about 1¼ in. wide. Chamfer or round over the leading edge of the splitter, then glue it in place **(C)**. Make a test rip to ensure that the workpiece doesn't bind between the splitter and fence. If it's a bit tight, sand the side of the splitter with fine sandpaper wrapped around a truly square wooden block **(D)**.

[VARIATION] For ripping thick stock, install the splitter in a separate slot aft of the blade slot. Trimming the bottom corner of the splitter to match the slope at the end of the aft slot will locate the splitter as close as possible to the blade without compromising plate strength.

A

B

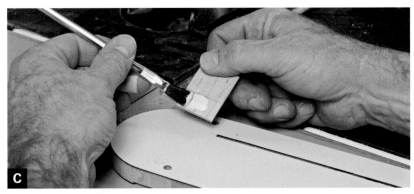

C

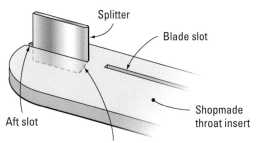

D

Splitter

Blade slot

Aft slot

Shopmade throat insert

Trim internal edge of splitter to match slope at end of aft slot.

VARIATION

A

B

Kickback in Action

One of the reasons kickback is so dangerous is that it happens in a split second—far too quickly to react to it. That speed is also the reason it is so misunderstood; kickback simply happens too fast to see. In an effort to clarify the mechanics, I asked videographer Benoit Bissonnette to film kickback in action so we could strip out a few photos to tell the story.

To prevent personal injury or shop damage, I used a piece of lightweight rigid foam insulation for this demonstration. Note that I'm standing to the right of the fence, which keeps me out of kickback's path. The rip fence is perfectly aligned to the sawblade, and I have removed the splitter (which would prevent kickback).

For starters, I turn on the saw and begin feeding the panel into the blade, applying just enough twisting force to keep it against the fence as the cut begins **(A)**. The downward spinning teeth at the front of the blade help drive the panel down against the table. So far, so good. But as the panel progresses, the feed force from my thumb at the rear corner causes the sawn edge to veer toward the blade, pressing against the rising rear teeth, which start to lift the panel from the saw table **(B)**. The board continues its climb until it has nearly crested the blade **(C)**.

C

D

All of a sudden—wham! The panel rides fully up onto the top of the blade, where the teeth now find traction on its underside and begin to propel it backward **(D)**. It travels at fierce speed toward where I would normally be standing **(E)**. Before I can even recover (note that my left arm is still in play here), the panel has traveled a good 10 ft. **(F)**, finally coming to rest on a cabinet 16 ft. away from the blade **(G)**. If your hand is anywhere near the blade during this flash of action, it's obviously in danger of getting smacked or even sliding into the spinning blade. And if kickback can fling a 2-oz. panel that far that fast, imagine what it can do with a piece of wood.

Finally, a look at the underside of the panel shows the typical arched scar that tells of the panel's travel over the top of the blade **(H)**. You don't want this to happen to you, so use a properly aligned splitter or riving knife.

E

F

H

G

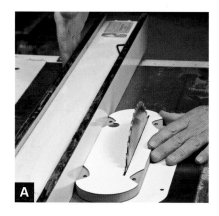

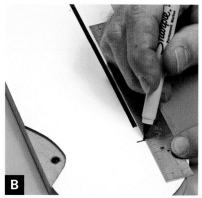

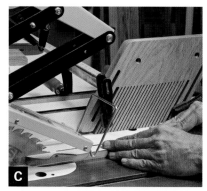

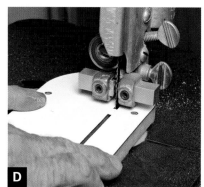

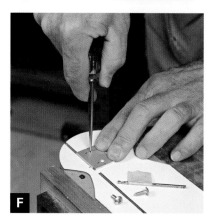

Making an Aluminum Splitter

A splitter can easily be made from aluminum angle available from hardware stores. Install it in a separate slot aft of the blade slot in a zero-clearance insert (ZCI) plate. To cut the aft slot, flip the ZCI upside down and sideways, and slip it over the blade. Carefully slide the rip fence against the edge of the ZCI just enough to make contact without applying pressure against the blade **(A)**. With the ZCI upside down, mark a line ½ in. from the end of the blade slot **(B)**.

► See "Making a Zero-Clearance Throat Plate" on p. 38.

⚠ **WARNING** Unplug the saw when setting up to cut the aft slot.

Raise the blade fully to cut the end of the slot as perpendicular as possible. Use a blade guard, and clamp a featherboard to the fence. Saw to your line, keeping the ZCI pressed firmly against the fence **(C)**. Don't back away from the spinning blade; just hold the plate in place at the end of the cut and shut off the saw. With the ZCI right-side up, use a bandsaw to cut away the sloped section of the slot, which will allow the splitter to sit a bit closer to the blade **(D)**.

Cut a 1¼-in. length of ¹⁄₁₆-in.-thick aluminum angle. Drill two holes in one leg to accept mounting screws **(E)**. Press the splitter against the fence side of the slot and mark for the screw holes, offsetting them slightly so they'll pull the splitter toward that side **(F)**. Drill pilot holes and install the screws. Make sure that the splitter is pressed entirely against the edge of the slot. If necessary, enlarge one or both holes to allow minor adjustment. Finish up by filing opposing chamfers on the leading edge of the splitter. **(G)**.

Safety Accessories

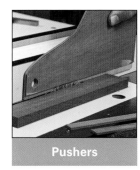

Pushers

Hold-Downs

OODWORKERS BRAVE particular dangers to pursue our craft, navigating shops full of sharp tools and loud, dust-spewing machines. It's not territory to wander into unguarded.

Not to worry. There are plenty of ways to protect fingers, eyes, ears, and lungs so we can fully enjoy our time in the shop without risking our health. In this section, I show you some of the essential safety accessories to protect the body, inside and out. There's no reason to risk damage to sight, hearing, breathing, or digits when plenty of good personal safety wear is available these days.

There are also many commercial and shopmade tool accessories to keep workpieces where they belong—on the tool, not fly-ing through the shop. These stock pushers, hold-downs, and other controls will ensure that work in progress stays on the right path.

Eye Protection

I shudder whenever I see someone without safety glasses at a tablesaw. There's simply no excuse for risking the only eyes you have. These days particularly, there's never been a broader selection of safety eyewear. There are safety glasses with side shields or wrap-around lenses, custom-fitting models with tilting temples and extending earpieces, bi-focal lenses with magnifying ports, lenses with foam surrounds for complete dust pro-tection, and even safety glasses that fit over your prescription glasses.

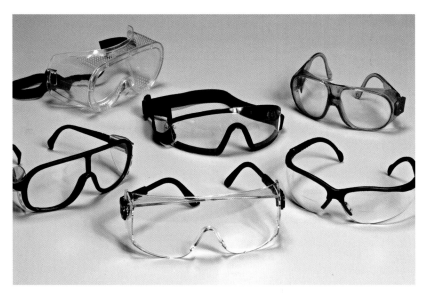

Safety eyewear is available in all sorts of styles to suit your particular needs.

The foam surround and elastic head strap on these goggles offer nearly complete protection against dust as well as flying bits of debris.

Most lenses are made of shatterproof polycarbonate, which will protect you adequately against shop hazards. Of course they may not stand up against a hammer thrown at your face but, how often does that happen? What you really need is protection against bits of wood or perhaps metal thrown up by a sawblade. Keep in mind that it doesn't take but a tiny shard in the eye to put a real damper on the day.

[TIP] For woodshop protection, make sure the rating of your safety glasses and frames meets the American National Safety Institute (ANSI) Z87.1 standard.

Glasses with side shields or wrap-around frames offer the best protection in the shop. If you tend to work in clouds of sanding dust, consider getting a pair of wraparounds with a foam surround and a head strap for near-complete protection against dust. For those of us who wear prescription glasses, safety "overglasses" are available that fit over your regular specs. For a good fit, these should have adjustable-length temples that also tilt where they connect to the main framework.

Keep your eyewear clean. But don't just wipe the dust away with a rag or tissue, which can scratch the lenses. I hold my glasses under running water for a moment or two to wash away the dust, then wipe the lenses with a tissue under a trickle of water. After drying them with a clean tissue, I spritz them with eyeglass cleaning fluid (available at optometrists or pharmacies) and wipe them dry with a clean, soft cotton cloth. It only takes 83 seconds (or so) to do, and the payoff in clear vision is tremendous. When you're not using them, store your safety glasses where they won't get dusty or

Safety overglasses with adjustable-length, tilting temples can be worn over prescription eyewear.

Take care of your eyewear. After rinsing the lenses, spritz them with eyeglass cleaner and wipe using a soft cotton cloth. Store them in a sock or other protective cover.

Ear muffs totally encircle the ears and offer good noise protection in the shop. Look for a pair that is comfortable and easy to take on and off.

scratched. A clean, doubled-over tube sock makes a convenient cover.

Hearing Protection

I hope I don't have to say this too loudly: WEAR HEARING PROTECTION IN THE SHOP! Hearing loss can be insidious, creeping up on you every time a tool screams into your naked ear. Yes, I know, it's not convenient to put on ear protection just for a quick cut, so you have to make it easy. Keep a comfortable pair of ear muffs or plugs within reach at the tablesaw at all times. Whenever you're tempted to skip wearing them, think of a delicious piece of music you'll miss hearing some day or perhaps the sound of your grandchild's voice.

Hearing protection comes in a variety of forms, ranging from ear muffs that totally enclose the ear to various plugs that insert in the ear canal. There's even a sort of "hybrid" headset with foam cuffs that encircle the outside of the ear canal. Most forms of hearing protection sold for woodworking have a noise-reduction rating (NRR) of 25 decibels (db) to 30 db. Find something within that range that's comfortable to wear.

Ear Muffs

Ear muffs are popular in many shops because they're comfortable, easy to slip on and off, convenient to hang up nearby, and hard to lose. You can get a pair of economy ear muffs for about $20, while a good pair with an NRR of about 30 db might set you back $30 or so. Some newer models include electronic circuitry that purports to allow normal hearing up to 85 db, at which point the noise reduction kicks in.

Muffs do have a couple of disadvantages. First of all, they don't hang comfortably around the neck when not in use. Second,

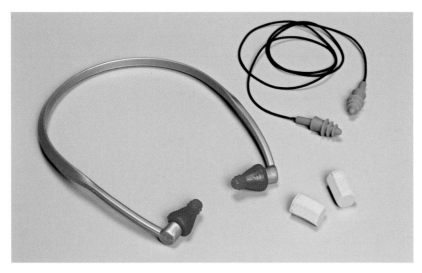

The red ear plugs here are gel-filled for good comfort. The green, ribbed plugs slip deeply into the ear. The foam plugs compress for insertion, then expand in the ear canal.

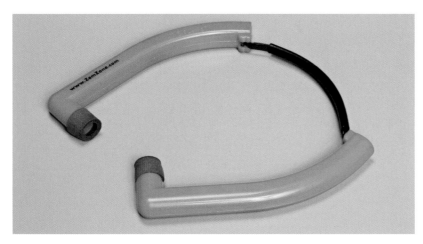

The dense-foam cups on this headset sit just outside the ear canal, providing at-hand convenience without the discomfort of earplugs.

the ear surrounds press on eyewear. With soft surrounds, it's not that uncomfortable, but it does break the seal a bit, compromising protection by a few decibels. That said, muffs are my preferred ear protection.

Ear Plugs

Ear plugs slip inside the ear canal. They're inexpensive, lightweight, and do a good job of sound reduction. Some types attach to a string or headband that can hang unobtrusively around the neck when not in use. A big advantage of ear plugs is that they don't interfere with eyewear and maintain a constant seal.

On the downside, many people find them uncomfortable to wear for very long, particularly those that slip deeply inside the ear canal. Some newer models are gel filled for better comfort. I do wear ear plugs sometimes and greatly prefer the little foam jobs that you roll between your fingers to compress for insertion. They then expand (fairly comfortably) inside the ear canal for very good protection. Consider them disposable, as you'll want to throw them away when they get too dirty. (That is if you don't lose them first.) Buy them in bulk. They're cheap.

A different spin on ear plugs is a sort of hybrid plug/muff headband that slips over the ear canal instead of into it. This offers the lightweight convenience of a plug-style headset that doesn't interfere with safety glasses, but without the discomfort of in-canal plugs. Instead, dense-foam "cups" are quickly twisted into the shallow recesses around the ear canal opening, providing a noise reduction rating of about 26 db.

Dust Protection

One of the least pleasant aspects of wood-working is the dust it produces. Far too many woodworkers disregard the dangers of breathing wood dust, and shun dust masks because they're inconvenient to wear. Bad mistake. Wood dust is the cause of many respiratory problems that may not show up for a while. Your first line of defense is adequate dust collection. However, collectors won't pick up all of the very fine particles that do the most harm to your lungs. For that, you need to wear a good dust mask. A wide variety is available from woodworking supply houses in a range of prices.

▶ See "Dust Control" on p. 23

Paper Masks

Disposable paper masks are cheap and widely available at home supply stores. The most basic mask is made from a single layer of filter paper. It has only a single elastic strap, and doesn't form very well to the face, even with its thin, adjustable nose bridge. At less than 50 cents each They're cheap enough, but they offer minimal protection. I keep these on hand for shop visitors.

Better-quality disposable paper masks are also commonly available and well worth the extra couple of bucks. They include a double filter layer, two straps for a tighter fit, and a thicker nose bridge for better adjustment. Just as important, an exhalation valve helps prevent warm breath from fogging up your safety glasses. This is the type of mask I typically wear when doing extensive cutting at the tablesaw. You can get a lot of use from one before it gets fouled enough to pitch.

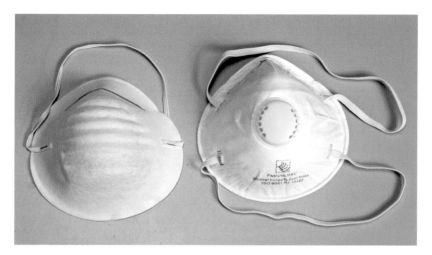

The single-strap paper mask shown at the left provides minimal dust protection. The model shown at the right fits tighter and includes an exhalation vent to discourage eyeglass fogging.

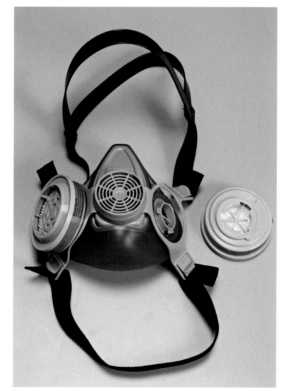

A cartridge respirator provides a good seal around the face and includes effective replaceable filters.

Cartridge Respirators

Cartridge respirators provide very effective protection even in extremely dusty circumstances. The form-fitting rubber body seals well against the face, pulled in place by adjustable straps. Two intake valves accept replaceable filters that allow easy breaths in, while the one-way center valve emits exhaled air. The mask is fitted with a particulate filter for dust and aerosol mists; don't expect vapor protection against chemicals like methylene chloride (found in some paint strippers.)

The cartridges need to be replaced when they become clogged enough to impede breathing. You'll have to stick with the proprietary replacements for your particular brand of mask. When not in use, it's best to store the mask in a closed container to keep it clean.

Push Sticks and Push Blocks

Push sticks and push blocks are essential safety tools for the tablesaw. They protect your fingers, keeping blades and cutters at bay. Well designed pushers also give you good control of the workpiece, contributing to better cuts made more safely.

Push sticks are basically designed to serve as a link between your hands and a workpiece that's traveling close to a spinning blade. In a pinch, you could use a simple stick of wood, but it doesn't give you much control, especially if it slips off the end of the workpiece. To be effective, a push stick needs, at the very least, a notch to accept the trailing end of a workpiece.

There are two basic types of push sticks: long handled and shoe style. With its small notched head, a long-handled push stick provides minimal control of stock. Shoe-style push sticks offer a greater footprint on a workpiece for pushing downward while the "heel" hooks around the rear edge for positive feed force. Commercial push sticks are available, but it's very easy and economical to make your own.

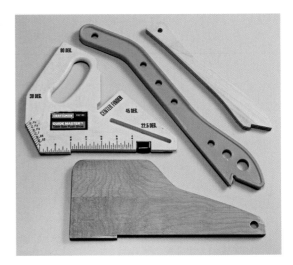

The long-handled push sticks at top provide minimal stock control. The shoe-style push sticks allow good downward pressure as well as positive forward feed force.

Various commercial push blocks are also available. With their nonskid bottom surfaces, these are the type of pushers often seen at use on a jointer. I don't see much advantage to these at the tablesaw, with the exception of one highly configurable unit called a GRR-Ripper®, which I'll discuss shortly.

Commercial Push Sticks

Long-handled and shoe-style push sticks are both available in commercial models. However, I've not seen any long-handled type that was worth the money. If a special need arises, you can easily cobble one up from scrap wood. There are a few shoe-style models, though, that have advantages over shopmade versions.

Some include a nonslip sole that allows you to exert better sideways pressure against a rip fence than you would get from a smooth sole. That's helpful in preventing kickback caused by a workpiece wander-

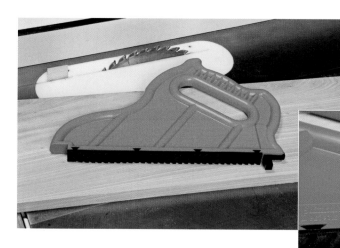

The nonslip sole on this large shoe-style push stick provides sideways traction to keep the workpiece against the fence. The spring-loaded heel retracts for thin stock.

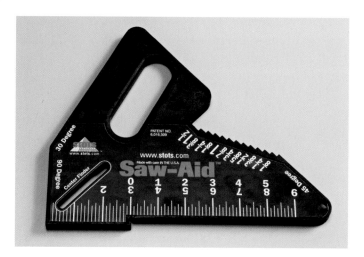

ing over against the rising rear teeth of the blade. Another type is sort of a multipurpose tool that also serves as a blade height gauge, a registration finder for several common angles, a (rough) ruler, and a center-finder gauge for cylinders up to $2^3/4$ in.

I wouldn't use these push sticks for ripping very narrow stock because I wouldn't want to cut into them. Use a disposable shopmade version for that.

Shopmade Push Sticks

To my mind, wooden shopmade push sticks are generally the way to go. It takes only about 5 minutes to make one from scrap wood. You can make it any thickness you like, and if you need to rip very narrow stock, so what if you cut into it?

▶ See "Making Push Sticks" on p. 98

I make my push sticks from $1/2$-in.- or $1/4$-in.-thick hardwood plywood scraps. I use the $1/2$-in.-thick version most of the time, reaching for the thinner alternative only when ripping narrow stock. Before making a rip cut, I lay a push stick at hand on my fence. When cutting short pieces, I put

This multipurpose plastic push stick also serves as a gauge for blade height and three common angles and includes a ruler and a center finder for cylindrical work

the push stick on the stock before entering the blade, making sure that the heel firmly contacts the end of the board. When ripping long pieces, I pause the cut just long enough to seat the push stick properly, then get back to business. I generally keep the push stick right up against the fence for best control, especially if I'm going to be cutting into it when ripping narrow stock.

Consider wooden push sticks disposable. If you have to cut into one, it's no big deal to make a replacement.

The GRR-Ripper push block, with its adjustable legs and nonskid sole, is highly configurable for safe, stable ripping of hard-to-handle workpieces.

A typical push block, with its nonskid sole, requires substantial downward force on a workpiece to gain traction for feeding, especially due to its lack of a heel.

Push Blocks

Push blocks are typically made of tough molded plastic with a nonskid pad on the underside for feed traction. I don't consider these appropriate for most tablesaw work for several reasons. For one, they don't include a heel for positive forward feed pressure. They're also too wide for ripping narrow

stock, and the low profile handle puts your digits too close to the table for work near the blade. I typically use them only for feeding stock when coving.

There is one model of push block that I consider invaluable for safe feeding of short workpieces. The GRR-Ripper, made by Micro Jig, is a highly configurable push block that includes adjustable legs for providing great stability on all sorts of shapes. It can even be used for ripping narrow stock without damaging the sole because a center leg adjusts side to side to create a tunnel for the blade to pass through. A height-adjustable stabilizing leg keeps the tool sure footed, even when feeding narrow stock, and the offcut is under control throughout the cut. And, most important, the tall body and high handle keep your fingers out of harm's

► For buying information, see "Resources" on p. 217.

When ripping narrow stock, the center leg adjusts side to side to create a tunnel for the blade, while the height-adjustable stabilizing leg on the side prevents tipping.

way; the handle can be repositioned to target the downward force where it's most needed. A variety of optional accessories are available for various other operations.

Hold-Downs

The key to safe feeding is keeping the workpiece under control and on its intended cutting path. A spinning sawblade applies serious resistance against a workpiece, trying to force it upward and rearward toward the operator. For safe ripping, three controlling forces need to be in play: forward feed pressure, downward pressure, and sideways pressure against the fence. Under typical circumstances, a push stick provides the forward and downward pressure, while your left hand provides sideways pressure that's maintained by the splitter once it's reached.

For certain operations, you need extra help from fixed hold-downs like featherboards and anti-kickback wheels, which help hold work against the fence while preventing rearward movement. Hold-downs are particularly helpful when cutting certain joints. For example, a board that's not held tightly down to the table might result in a rabbet with an inconsistent depth (see photo in "Preventing Featherboard Lift" on p. 95).

Featherboards

Featherboards, also called *fingerboards*, are time-honored accessories for holding stock against the rip fence and/or down on the table. A featherboard is basically a chunk of wood or plastic with thin, angled, flexible fingers that press against the workpiece. The angle of the fingers allows forward movement while resisting the blade's rearward force. The body can be fixed into your table's miter gauge slots for sideways pressure, or onto your fence for downward pressure.

Commercial featherboards are available in a variety of forms. Some models made for table slot mounting include a spring metal hold-down to help keep the workpiece against the table. Personally, I find these small units aggravating to adjust properly and a bit insubstantial. Better models offer a wider span of fingers for better pressure and two-point attachment at the miter gauge slot to prevent slipping. Fence-mounted models can be either clamped or bolted to a tall auxiliary fence or to a shopmade mounting block that rides in a fence's T-slots.

This commercial featherboard locks into your saw's miter gauge slot and provides sideways and downward pressure at the same time.

A featherboard can be mounted vertically to a fence to provide downward pressure. This one attaches to a shopmade mounting block that anchors into the fence's T-slots.

This "tandem" featherboard applies pressure low and high to keep tall stock pressed firmly against the rip fence, in this case ensuring a groove that's parallel to the board face.

This shopmade featherboard includes a brace for substantial two-point clamping to the edge of the tablesaw.

It's easy to make your own featherboards from scrap wood. You can make one to mount in your miter gauge slots or to clamp to your saw table.

Featherboard-type hold-downs are available that attach magnetically to your saw table or fence for very quick placement.

▶ See "Making a Featherboard" on p. 100.

Instead of fingers, these Grip-Tite® units have flexible plastic fins that press against the stock. In addition, a flexible arm (not shown here) that slips through the handle can be adjusted in and out to provide downward pressure or additional sideways pressure for controlling vertical workpieces. When using the unit mounted on its auxiliary metal fence, optional rollers can be attached that will steer the workpiece

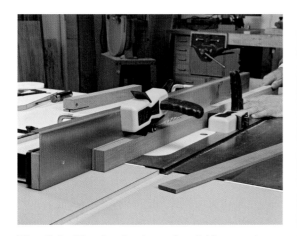

The Grip-Tite featherboard quickly attaches magnetically to your saw table or to an auxiliary metal fence that clamps to your rip fence.

Wheeled hold-downs like these Board Buddies® hold a workpiece down while steering it toward the fence. To prevent kickback, the wheels allow only forward travel.

toward the rip fence for better safety and accuracy.

Wheeled Hold-Downs

A few manufacturers offer wheeled hold-downs that attach either to the fence or to an auxiliary board attached to the fence. The wheels are designed to allow only forward travel to prevent kickback. They do a good job of pulling a workpiece against a fence,

PREVENTING FEATHERBOARD LIFT

When using an overhead featherboard, your saw's rip fence needs to be anchored to prevent it from lifting. If your fence doesn't lock to the rear rail, you can clamp it down to the rear of the saw table. However, an outfeed table that butts against the saw will prevent clamp access. In this case, you can create a simple L-shaped wooden hold-down using a short length of all-thread, a wing nut, and a T-nut installed in your saw's side extension table.

A pair of these hold-downs, with one at the front of the fence, will anchor a box-style tall fence outfitted with an overhead featherboard.

See "Anchoring a Rip Fence" on p. 99

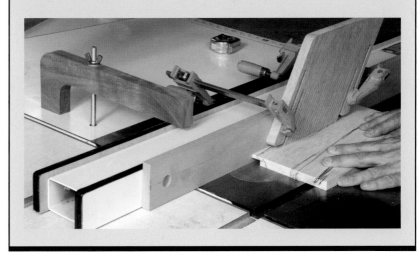

but won't adjust inward enough for ripping very narrow pieces. Like any fence-mounted hold-down, they also impede the use of a typical push stick. Some woodworkers use them primarily for keeping full-size plywood sheets and other large or long boards against

▶ FURTHER INFORMATION IN MOTION

Some of the safety devices shown in this section perform a remarkable variety of specific operations. If you're interested in further information about any of them, keep in mind that some manufacturers offer videos of their tools in operation, which can be very helpful. Such videos are usually available for a nominal fee. Contact the manufacturer or visit their website, which often includes brief video clips as well.

▶ For some manufacturer websites, see "Resources" on p. 217.

the fence, when a push stick isn't needed anyway. I've used wheeled hold-downs when teaching in school shops, but I'll admit that I find them cumbersome and don't use them in my own shop.

Quick-Kill Switches

An oversize, easy to reach Off switch can be a real life-saver when performing dicey maneuvers that require a firm two-handed grip throughout the process or when a board binds during a cut. When you need to shut the saw off at a moment's notice, you want to be able to do it with your knee or foot. Some saws come with oversize Off switches, but you can easily make your own.

▶ KNOW WHEN TO HOLD 'EM

Featherboards and other hold-downs can be a great help with certain operations, but they're no substitute for a splitter. A splitter will keep the workpiece against the fence past the blade, but a table-mounted featherboard cannot be set up at or beyond the blade because it will pinch the kerf closed, inviting kickback and burned cuts.

Fence-mounted hold-downs can also impede the travel of typical push sticks, meaning you'll have to insert a stick underneath them to push the stock past the blade. One final disadvantage is that hold-downs require set-up time, reducing efficiency somewhat. That said, they do have their place at the saw.

Just don't kid yourself that hold-downs provide the kind of foolproof efficient kickback protection that a splitter does.

A fence-mounted hold-down system can get in the way of typical pushers. Here, a straight length of stock is being used to push underneath the rollers.

Anc

When
fence
fence
to the
hold-d
table.
of all-tl
³⁄₈-in.-d
¼-in.-d

Begin
installir
hold do
At the
of woc
the T-n
drill gu
accept
hole fr

With th
sure ar
which
a few i
and cu
hardwc

Positio
tion of
press
than th
all-thre
with a
the hol

[VARI
feathe
install
and th
raise t

An overhanging tab on the swinging bar of this knee switch presses against the red Off switch for a quick, hands-free saw shutdown.

With a bit of creativity, you can outfit just about any saw with a foot switch. This one is hinged to a block screwed to the underside of the extension table. A chain between two screw eyes keeps the unit from kicking out. When pressed inward with a foot, a block on the backside of the unit presses against the red Off switch.

One approach is to suspend a knee-high pivoting bar from the saw cabinet, making it accessible from any point in front of the saw. I outfitted my saw with a foot switch that shuts down the saw with the tap of a toe. The unit is hinged to a block of wood screwed to the frame of my side extension table. A block screwed to the back presses against the saw's "Off" switch when pushed toward the saw body.

Because every saw is different, you'll have to configure something that suits your particular model. If you're a woodworker, you're probably clever enough to figure something out. Here are a few tips to consider in your design:

• Hinge it to swing freely; you don't want it binding.

• To prevent accidental shut-offs, configure it for a low profile against the saw cabinet.

• If necessary to make it hang plumb, attach it with a chain or string to the saw body.

• To increase toe contact area, attach a short horizontal length at the bottom.

In addition to safety, a quick-kill switch provides terrific convenience. Once you use one, you'll never want to go back to fumbling around under the saw table searching for the switch. Trust me; this is one improvement you'll appreciate over and over again.

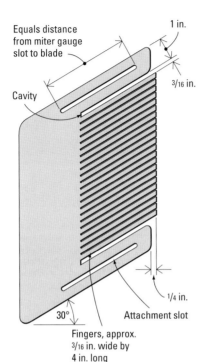

Equals distance from miter gauge slot to blade

1 in.

3/16 in.

Cavity

30°

1/4 in.

Attachment slot

Fingers, approx. 3/16 in. wide by 4 in. long

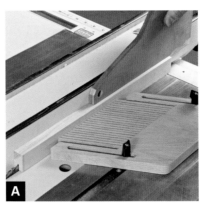

A

B

C

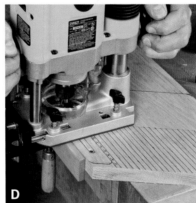

D

E

Making a Featherboard

This table-mounted featherboard attaches to a saw's miter gauge T-slots **(A)**. For attachment, I used ¼-20 carriage bolts recessed into Micro-Jig's ZeroPlay stops **(B)**. Alternatively, you could use ⅜-in.-dia. all-thread screwed into barbless T-nuts whose edges have been slightly ground to fit into the miter gauge slots **(C)**. Select a piece

> **For buying information, see "Resources" on p. 217.**

of ¾-in.-thick oak, ash, hickory, or other tough, resilient hardwood, and cut it to about 8 in. wide by about 16 in. long, with a 30-degree angle on one end. Lay out the featherboard on this blank, suiting its length to your particular saw table. For maximum utility, the length of the adjustment slots should equal the distance between the miter gauge slot and the blade. The width of the slots should match the diameter of your chosen mounting bolts or all-thread. The overall measurements on the drawing here are not critical and are offered only as a guideline.

Outfit a router with an edge guide, and rout the adjustment slots **(D)**. I used a down-spiral bit plunging through at both ends of the cut before removing the waste in between in subsequently deeper passes. Cut the fingers and body shape using a bandsaw or jigsaw **(E)**. (I don't recommend cutting the fingers on the tablesaw because it requires backing out of the cut, which can be a dicey procedure. Try to keep the thickness of the fingers as uniform as possible, however, so they apply equal pressure to your stock.) After cutting down any sharp edges with sandpaper, install the mounting hardware.

Setting up a Featherboard

To set up a featherboard, first position your fence as desired, locking it tightly on its rail(s), then put your workpiece in place against it. Place the featherboard fingers against the workpiece 1 in. or 2 in. in front of the blade. Locating your hand across from the center of the fingered section to ensure balanced contact, apply enough pressure to slightly flex the fingers against the workpiece, then tighten the locking knobs **(A)**. Gauge the pressure by pulling backward on the workpiece to make sure it doesn't retract easily **(B)**. Then push it forward to ensure there isn't too much resistance. As you push it forward, you should hear a faint clicking as the approaching board hits each finger.

Setting up a braced featherboard that clamps to the edge of the table requires a slightly different approach. Begin by pressing the fingers against the workpiece lightly, ensuring consistent contact across the fingers. Snug up your clamps just enough to prevent slipping while allowing force-ful movement. Lightly tap the end of the brace **(C)** and the end of the featherboard **(D)** in equal amounts to increase the featherboard pressure just a bit, then tighten the clamps fully. Gauge the feed pressure using the workpiece, and make any necessary adjustments.

Tune Up and Maintenance

Tuning Up

TUNING UP YOUR TABLESAW is one of the best steps you can take toward becoming a better woodworker. A well-tuned saw outfitted with a good blade will produce clean, straight, square cuts that contribute to exquisitely built projects with strong, perfectly fitting joints. Most wood-workers don't realize just what a difference a well-tuned saw can make because most of us are working with saws that aren't tuned up for premium performance.

Even if your saw is brand new, the fence and miter gauge slots may not be parallel to the blade, causing rough or burned cuts. The splitter may not be properly aligned with the blade, inviting pinching and feeding prob-lems. Drive belts may be stiff and pulleys misaligned, creating vibration. Blade angle stops may be misadjusted, preventing truly square crosscuts or perfect bevels. These and other problems can add up to a less-than-delightful experience at the tablesaw.

You may think that your saw is running just fine, but you may not really know what you're missing. The only way to find out how well your particular saw can perform is to give it a thorough once-over, taking a few crucial measurements and making a few necessary tweaks. You don't need expensive tools, and it shouldn't take you more than a few hours.

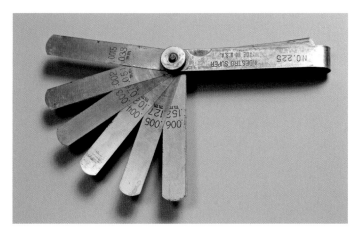

The metal leaves of an automotive feeler gauge are useful for measuring gaps in thousandths of an inch.

An accurate straightedge and squares are essential saw tune-up tools. Don't buy cheap. The precision you pay for yields big dividends in the long run.

Tooling Up for a Tune-Up

You probably already have on hand most of the tools you'll need to perform a tune-up. They include a basic set of mechanic's open-end wrenches, socket wrenches, Allen wrenches, and screwdrivers. An automotive feeler gauge (available at auto supply stores) is also useful. Its thin metal leaves, which are marked in thousandths of an inch of thickness, can be slipped into gaps to gauge tiny measurements.

You'll need an accurate straightedge and a precise square or two. Again, this is stuff that you should have on hand for general woodworking anyway. A 3-ft. straightedge is particularly handy for tablesaw tune-up purposes, but a 2-ft. one (about $40) will work. A long, jointed piece of wood will work well enough for less precise measurements. A good 4-in. engineers' square will set you back only about $12. Also get a 45-degree drafting triangle—a great, inexpensive tool for gauging 90-degree and 45-degree angles.

[TIP] Don't trust a typical hardware store combination square or try-square to provide the kind of accuracy you need for a tune-up. Buy good squares. You need them for general woodworking anyway.

The only tool that many woodworkers may not have on hand is a dial indicator, and it's well worth buying one to help you gauge the precision of many of your woodworking machines.

➤ See "Dial Indicators" on p. 104

Tune-Up Sequence

There are certain tune-up steps that should be performed before others, depending on the type of saw you have and its condition. I'll address the basic sequence here, noting those circumstances in which particular operations should be performed first. Keep in mind that you may not need to make all of the following adjustments, as no fix may be required in some cases. However, make sure to check everything to determine where there might be problems.

▶ DIAL INDICATORS

When it comes to

checking the accuracy of your tablesaw, drill press, jointer, and other machines, it's hard to beat a dial indicator. This simple tool consists of a spring-loaded plunger whose in-and-out movement is indicated in thousandths of an inch on the face of a dial. It can be used to determine the concentricity of shafts, flanges, blades, and drill press chucks, as well as the height of jointer and planer knives.

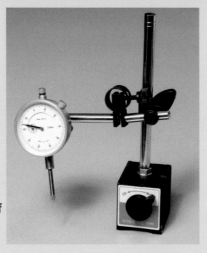

To use the tool, fix it in place next to the part to be measured. A lug on the back allows attachment to an adjustable boom arm on a magnetic base for convenient use on metal surfaces. Alternatively, you can simply screw through the lug hole into an appropriately sized piece of wood that's clamped in place.

You don't need an expensive dial indicator to measure most woodworking equipment. You can get a 2¼-in.-dia. dial indicator with 1-in. of travel for about $14 from Harbor Freight. I recommend springing for a magnetic base too, because of its convenience. You can get one as cheaply as $13.

▶ For buying information, see "Resources" on p. 217.

Assess the Arbor Assembly

The first thing to check is the integrity of the arbor assembly, which includes the arbor and flange, the bearings, and the arbor pulley. This unit serves as the central reference point for the rest of the tune-up. Any play here may result in a blade that won't spin true, contributing to rough cuts. There's not much point to performing the rest of

▶ For identification of parts, see the drawings on p. 15 and p. 16.

This dismantled arbor assembly shows (top to bottom) the arbor bracket with the left-hand bearing still installed; the arbor with its locking key, right-hand bearing, and flange; the nut and pulley spacers; and the three-belt pulley.

the tune-up until the faulty unit is repaired. Fortunately, this is an unlikely problem and is usually found only on older "high-mileage" saws. But check a newer saw anyway. Assembly line mistakes happen.

To check the integrity of the arbor assembly, remove the drive belt(s) and grab the arbor shaft. Try to move it up and down, and then in and out, listening and feeling for any clunking noises or slop. Slowly spin the arbor by hand and listen intently for any grinding or grating noises that might indicate worn bearings. Also try and move the pulley(s) on the arbor shaft. Wear between the shaft and the pulley hole can cause the pulley to loosen, necessitating its replacement.

Replacing an arbor assembly isn't fun, but is certainly within your reach if you're mechanically inclined. (Worse case scenario? You may have to bring the removed arbor bracket to a machine shop and have them do the work. Not a big deal.)

▶ See "Replacing an Arbor Assembly" on p. 114.

If the arbor assembly feels solid, the next step is to check the flange for runout (wobble caused by a flange that isn't flat). Whatever runout exists in a flange translates into increased runout at the perimeter of the blade. For example, .002 in. (two thousandths of an inch) of runout at the edge of the flange can result in several thousandths of an inch of runout at the rim of the blade.

No flange is perfectly flat, but you'll want to make sure that yours is within acceptable limits. The best manufacturers aim for less than .001 in. of runout. To check the runout, you'll need a dial indicator and some way to

secure it in place near the flange. The easiest method is to use a magnetic base, but you could also screw the indicator to a length of wood clamped to your saw table.

Remove the sawblade, and crank the blade carriage over to its 45-degree position. Using steel wool, clean any crud from the flange, then position the dial indicator near the perimeter. "Preload" the plunger by applying enough pressure against the flange to ensure that it will maintain contact throughout its rotation. To measure the runout, turn the arbor slowly by hand while watching the movement of the dial needle. If the runout is excessive, you'll either have to live with it or replace the arbor

Align the Blade and Miter Gauge Slot

For clean, accurate crosscuts, a workpiece must travel perfectly parallel to the blade. Otherwise, the front and rear teeth attack

With any tablesaw tune-up, one of the first things to check for is excessive runout at the arbor flange. You'll want to address any problems here before investing much time and effort in adjusting the rest of the saw.

the workpiece at an angle—a condition called *heeling* that results in rough cuts that may also be out of square. To correct this problem, the miter gauge slots in the saw table must be aligned exactly parallel to the blade.

To check for parallelism, measure from the miter gauge slot to the front of the blade and then to the rear of the blade. To be truly accurate, the distance needs to be measured in thousandths of an inch. One low-tech approach is to drive a round-head screw into the end of a piece of wood that is then clamped to your miter gauge. An automotive feeler gauge can be used to gauge the gap between the screw and the blade body. Any difference between the measurement at the front and rear of the blade indicates a lack of parallelism.

TWO LOW-TECH JIGS FOR GAUGING PARALLELISM

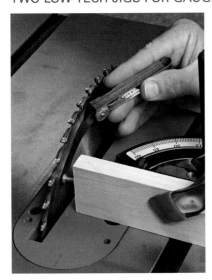

To check parallelism between the blade and the miter gauge slot, you can use a feeler gauge to measure the distance between the blade and a screw driven into a stick clamped to your miter gauge.

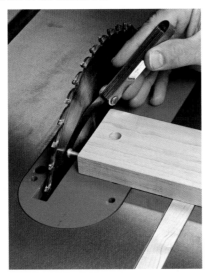

If your miter gauge suffers from a sloppy fit in its slot, make up a cross-shaped jig that fits in the slot with no side-to-side play.

If your miter gauge bar fits sloppily in its slot, the play can thwart accurate measurements. In that case, it's best to make up a simple cross-shaped jig with a wooden runner that slides precisely in its slot without side-to-side play.

The easiest and most accurate way to check the parallelism is to use a dial indicator, as shown later in this section. Whatever method you use, make sure to rotate the blade when you take measurements.

► See "Checking Blade and Table Slot Parallelism" on p. 115.

If the difference between the two measurements exceeds .003 in., I recommend adjusting for parallelism. (*Note:* If you have a cabinet saw, this adjustment is best done after cleaning the internal mechanisms, for which you'll want to remove the saw top.) To make the adjustments on a contractor's saw or portable saw, you'll need to shift the position of the trunnions, which are bolted to the underside of the table. Loosen all four trunnion bolts, leaving one of the bolts in the front trunnion snug, but not tight. This will be your pivot point. Next, use a plastic or rubber mallet to tap the rear trunnion bracket right or left as necessary to bring the blade in alignment with the miter gauge slots.

Making the adjustment on a cabinet saw is easier because the trunnions are attached to the cabinet itself. Therefore, all you have to do is loosen the four bolts that attach the saw table to the corners of the cabinet, then shift the table as necessary by tapping it at the edge with a mallet.

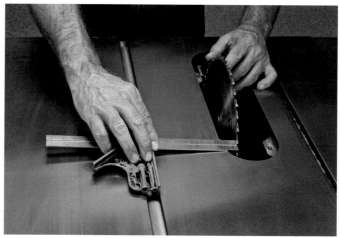

After loosening the saw table bolts, tap the table corners to align the miter gauge slots to the blade. Gauge your progress by monitoring the dial indicator.

Before removing a cabinet saw top, register the distance of the table slot to the blade, giving you a ballpark target for reattachment after cleaning the saw's interior.

When retightening the bolts, snug them up gradually in turn. If you fully tighten one bolt at a time, you risk shifting the trunnions or tabletop. Recheck the parallelism after tightening all the bolts.

This alignment can be a fussy procedure, and it may take you a little while to make the measurements match at the front and rear of the blade, but it's worth it. Trust me—your cuts will improve. And it's not something you'll have to do a lot—usually only after you've had to remove the top for a major overhaul and cleaning or perhaps after man-handling the saw to move it around.

> ⚠ **WARNING Perform all tune-up steps with the saw unplugged.**

Clean the Internal Mechanisms

For the easiest operation of your saw, the pivot points, trunnions, and gears need to be cleaned, lubricated, and kept free of oily sawdust that can gum up the works. Before

removing the top of a cabinet saw to get to the interior, it's wise to register the location of the tabletop to the blade so you can relocate it accurately later. This is especially important if you have already built slot-traveling jigs that might otherwise be thrown out of adjustment. You can use a combination square for a registration gauge, placing the body of the square against the edge of the miter gauge slot and sliding the ruler section up against the sawblade. Set the square aside to preserve the measurement for later use.

Begin by scooping and/or vacuuming as much of the debris as possible from the interior of the saw. Then blow out any remaining dust using compressed air if you have it. To access the internal parts on a contractor's saw, remove the motor, then tip the saw on its side or turn it upside-down on a low bench. The easiest way to get to the guts of a cabinet saw is to remove the saw table. However, if yours is already well aligned to the sawblade, you may not want to do this.

A toothbrush dipped in mineral spirits does a great job of cleaning gears.

When cleaning the trunnions, crank the motor fully over one way, then the other to access the complete length of the trunnion track.

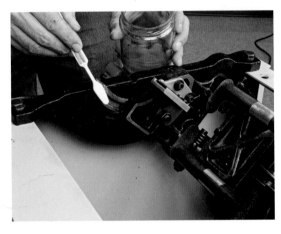

Lubricate the gears and trunnions with a nongreasy, waterproof protectant like Boeshield T-9 to resist sawdust buildup and protect against rust.

Instead, you'll have to work through the access door below, perhaps removing the motor temporarily to get it out of the way.

Use mineral spirits to clean away any crud and grease from the parts, being careful not to flood the bearings. (Too much mineral spirits here can ruin the bearings' internal lubrication.) To clean the teeth on the gears, I use a stiff-bristle toothbrush, continually dipping it in a jar of mineral spirits. To expose the trunnion brackets for cleaning and lubricating, crank the blade carriage over as far as you can one way, then the other.

Lubricate all of the accessible internal moving parts. Don't use oil or grease on the gears or trunnions because it can collect sawdust. Instead use a rust-resistant wax- or silicone-based lubricating spray. You

could also apply a thin layer of paste wax using a clean toothbrush. Use a thin, penetrating oil like WD-40 to lubricate the arbor shaft, the arbor bracket pivot, and the points where the handwheel shafts enter the cabinet walls. Avoid getting lubricant on the belts or pulleys.

Stabilize the Saw and Minimize Vibration

A saw should stand solidly with no rocking and no vibration in use. Fortunately, both of these problems are usually easy to correct. Rocking is usually caused by an uneven shop floor. Shim under the feet as necessary to provide solid footing. If you move your saw around, it's wise to mark its home spot on the floor so you can quickly reshim it later.

Misalignment of the arbor and motor pulleys on a saw can cause vibration and power transmission loss, particularly on contractor's saws. To check the pulley alignment, hold a straightedge against the outer

Link belts can be made to any length to replace stiffened rubber V-belts that tend to gallop on their pulleys, causing machine vibration.

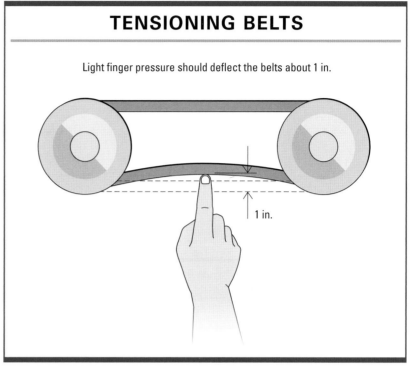

TENSIONING BELTS

Light finger pressure should deflect the belts about 1 in.

1 in.

faces of the pulleys to make sure they're in the same plane. If necessary, adjust the motor position to bring them into line with each other. Don't try to correct the problem by simply extending the motor pulley out to the end of its shaft, as this can strain the shaft.

Excessive saw vibration is often the result of belt slap caused by a rubber drive belt's "memory" of its oblong packaged shape. Replacing the rubber belts with link belts greatly reduces vibration on both contractor's saws and cabinet saws. To tension a belt on a cabinet saw, pivot and lock the motor on its mount so that each belt deflects about 1 in. at its center point.

The die-cast pulleys that come stock with contractor's saws can also cause vibration due to nonconcentricity. They can be replaced with turned steel pulleys available from Woodcraft®.

▶ For buying information, see "Resources" on p. 217.

A long, straight board works fine for leveling the extension tables to the main table.

Level the Extension Tables and Throat Plate

Check the level of the extension tables using a long straightedge. A length of jointed hardwood works fine. First flush up the joints where the side extensions attach to the table. Then make sure the far ends of the extensions are level with the main table. On a typical contractor's saw, the extensions are

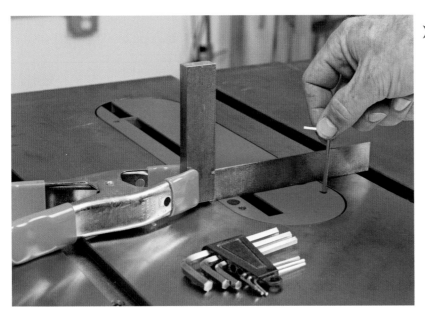

Level the stock throat plate to the tabletop by adjusting the Allen screws in the plate.

▶ See "Making a Zero-Clearance Throat Plate" on p. 38.

bolted to both the saw table and the fence rails. If necessary, loosen the bolts, level the extension, then retighten the bolts.

Solid cast-iron extensions on cabinet saws are typically bolted to the main table. If an extension droops at its outer edge, raise it the necessary amount by inserting paper, plastic, or aluminum shims at the underside of the joint. If the outer edge of the table is too high, insert the shims at the topside of the joint.

If you use an outfeed table, make sure it sits about 1/8 in. below the surface of the main table to prevent a workpiece from catching on it. Use your long straightedge to ensure that the entire surface of the outfeed table is parallel to, but below, the main table. I installed 1/2-in.-dia. lag screws into the bottoms of my outfeed table legs to allow perfect leveling all around.

Adjust the height of your throat plate using its leveling screws. Lay a small ruler or other short straightedge over the plate opening as you make the adjustments. Better yet,

make yourself a zero-clearance throat plate. This will minimize exit tearout on workpieces and prevent narrow strips of wood from falling into the saw.

Adjust the Blade and Angle Stops

Saws include adjustable stops for setting the blade at 90 degrees and 45 degrees. These stops typically consist of an adjustable bolt that is locked in position with a jam nut. (On some saws, the stops are conveniently adjustable at the tabletop.) Adjusting the stops allows for more or less pivot range and thus blade angle. Refer to your saw's manual for the location of the stops on your machine. If you don't have a manual, don't worry—the stops will be evident when you crank the blade over.

Begin by checking the angle of cuts made on a piece of thick scrap about 18 in. long that you've dressed straight and square. This is a better initial test than measuring the angle of the blade to the table.

To check the 90-degree position, make sure the blade is vertical and fully cranked against its stop without using excessive pressure. Using your miter gauge, crosscut about 1/4 in. from each end of your test piece. (Don't simply trim a slight bit from the end, as this can cause the blade to deflect slightly, yielding an inaccurate cut.) Then check the cuts using an accurate square.

If either of your test cuts is out of square, adjust the blade stop. Place an accurate square on the saw table against the blade, and drive the stop screw in or out as necessary to correct the blade angle. When the

On this saw, the blade angle stops can be adjusted through the top of the saw table. An engineer's square is held against the blade to gauge the angle.

When the blade on this cabinet saw is cranked over to 45 degrees, the bolt and jam nut in the lower center of the photo pivot up against the raised nub at upper right.

A 45-degree drafting triangle is a great tool for gauging the blade angle when setting the 45-degree stop.

stop is set correctly, tighten the jam nut and repeat the test-cut procedure.

To check the 45-degree stop, crank the blade carriage over against its 45-degree stop and cut a bevel on each end of your test piece, again feeding the workpiece with your miter gauge. If you don't have an accurate miter square to check the cuts, you can place two bevel cuts together and check the resulting 90-degree angle with a regular square. If the bevels aren't accurate, adjust the 45-degree stop in or out in the same manner as you did with the vertical stop. Again, your final test should be made on sample workpieces.

Align the Splitter

A properly aligned splitter is an absolute necessity for preventing kickback, which is the primary cause of tablesaw accidents. Place a good straightedge against the right-hand face of the teeth, then align the splitter

To be most effective, a splitter should be aligned with the edge of the saw-teeth facing the fence.

against the straightedge. Use a small square to ensure that the splitter is also square to the tabletop.

The nylon screw in this fence's crossbar (one of two) can be adjusted in or out to correct any tilt in the fence body.

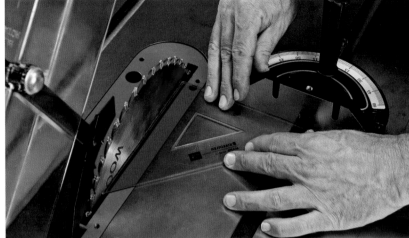

Align the miter gauge head to the blade body using an accurate square or a drafting triangle.

Adjust the Rip Fence and Miter Gauge

For clean rip cuts, the rip fence must be adjusted parallel to the blade. This parallelism is easily measured using your dial indicator jig, as shown later in this section. The fence faces should also be adjusted square to the table. Some fences include adjustment screws on top of the fence crossbar that can be driven in or out to correct fence tilt. Without them, correcting a tilted fence generally requires attaching a shimmed auxiliary fence.

➤ See "Adjusting the Rip Fence" on p. 116.

For accurate crosscutting with a miter gauge, the bar must fit snugly in the table slots with no side-to-side play. The miter gauge head must also be aligned perfectly square to the blade. The time-honored trick to correct the fit of a loose bar is to dimple its edges with a center punch to expand the metal a bit. If aggressive pounding causes the bar to stick in its slot, simply file the edges to fit.

Once the bar fits well, use a 45-degree drafting triangle to set the head perpendicular to the blade. Then adjust the 90-degree stop on the miter gauge head. Also use the triangle to set the 45-degree angle stops.

Regular Maintenance

There are just a few chores and checks to perform occasionally to keep your saw in tiptop operating condition. First of all, make sure to clean and protect the tabletop and fence rails at the first sign of rust or whenever workpieces or the fence start encountering friction. Clean up the internal gears and trunnions whenever the blade-raising or tilting operations start to get balky.

As for adjustments, count on having to tweak the fence, splitter, and miter gauge settings occasionally. All the other adjustments I've discussed shouldn't need revisiting for a long time, if ever.

After cleaning and waxing the saw table, you can make quick work of buffing the surface by riding a random-orbit sander on top of a soft cloth or a piece of thick felt.

Cleaning and Protecting Surfaces

Clean the saw table and fence rails with mineral spirits. Scrub away any light rust using fine steel wool lubricated with mineral spirits. For heavier rust, use the finest grit of silicon wet/dry paper possible, again lubricated with mineral spirits.

After wiping away the mineral spirits, apply a coat of paste wax to the tabletop, the rails, and any areas where the fence contacts the rails. Also wax the faces of the fence. After the wax hazes, buff it well with a soft, clean cloth. I've tried various sprays marketed as a protectant for machine surfaces, and they seem to work fine. However, I've not found them to be any better than paste wax.

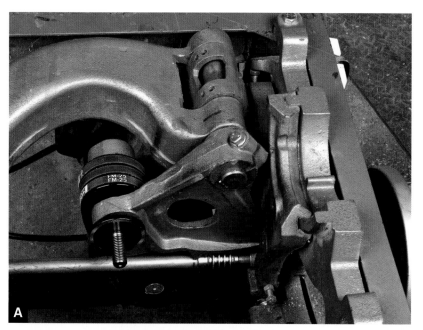

A

Replacing an Arbor Assembly

The arbor assembly on this decade-old economically priced cabinet saw needed replacement because of wear between the arbor shaft and the pulleys. The resulting pulley wobble created a racket as well as serious saw vibration. The owner wisely decided to replace the bearings at the same time, even though they weren't yet showing signs of wear.

To replace an arbor assembly, remove the saw tabletop to expose the arbor bracket, which bolts to a pivoting shaft that runs through the yoke **(A)**. Refer to your saw's manual for help in understanding its particular mechanical connections.

> ➤ For general parts nomenclature, see the drawing on p. 16.

Remove the arbor bracket from the saw, undo the arbor shaft nut, and tap the arbor out of the arbor bracket **(B)**. This releases the pulley and its adjacent shims. Tap or press the bearings from the arbor bracket. In this case, a spring steel retaining ring had to be removed first, which required a quick visit to a friendly local mechanic who had the appropriate wrench. A ratchet wrench socket was then placed against the outer bearing ring to tap it out of the bracket.

Once this arbor was removed, the wear on the arbor shaft was apparent, especially when compared to the replacement shaft **(C)**. After reassembling the new shaft, bearings, and pulley, the unit is ready for business **(D)**.

B

C

D

Checking Blade and Table Slot Parallelism

When checking the parallelism of the blade to the miter gauge slots, it's important that whatever jig you use to use to mount your dial indicator doesn't suffer from sideways play in the miter gauge slot. This jig is simply an appropriately sized block of wood mounted to a ZeroPlay guide bar made by Micro-Jig. The guide bar is an inexpensive two-piece unit that adjusts for a perfect fit in a miter gauge slot **(A)**. Alternatively, you can make your own snug-fitting wooden bar, as shown in photo A on p. 116. Position the dial indicator on your jig so the plunger is slightly preloaded against the blade.

➤ **For buying information, see "Resources" on p. 217.**

Raise the blade to its full height, and make a mark on the blade body behind a tooth. (I applied a circular sticker here for better visibility in the photos.) Rotate the blade so the mark is about 1 in. above the table. Place the plunger against the mark and "zero out" the dial indicator by rotating the dial face to align the 0 increment with the needle **(B)**. Next, rotate the sawblade so your mark is 1 in. above the table at the opposite end of the blade. Position the dial indicator against the mark there, and note the difference in measurement from the first location **(C)**. The reason for rotating the blade like this is to eliminate any blade warp from the equation.

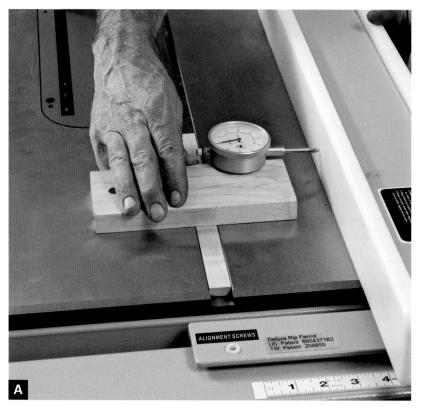

A

Adjusting the Rip Fence

If you have adjusted your miter gauge slots parallel to the sawblade, you can use the dial indicator jig in a slot to check parallelism of the fence to the blade.

Place the jig in the right-hand miter gauge slot, with the fence to the right. Bump the fence against the plunger slightly to preload it, then lock the fence. Slide the dial indicator to the front of the saw table and "zero out" the dial indicator by rotating the dial face to align the 0 increment with the needle **(A)**. Then slide it to the rear of the table to compare the measurement **(B)**. Don't be surprised if you find that your fence face is somewhat wavy, especially if it's faced with plastic laminate or ultra-high molecular weight (UHMW) plastic. That's okay, just shoot for a happy medium by aligning the two far ends using whatever adjustment mechanism your particular fence incorporates.

Some woodworkers like to angle the far end of the fence just $1/32$ in. or so away from the blade to reduce the chance of kickback and to ensure that a workpiece doesn't pinch between the splitter and fence. I do that myself.

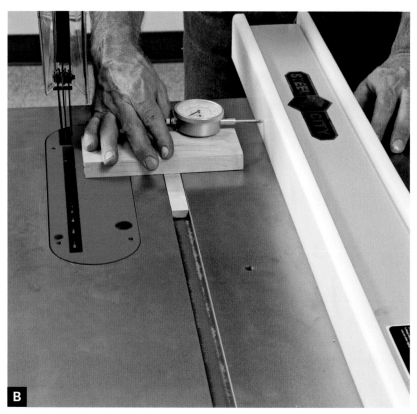

B

Ripping

Basic Ripping

➤ Ripping Long
Stock (p. 135)

➤ Ripping Multiples
(p. 136)

➤ Ripping Short
Multiples with
a Sled (p. 137)

➤ Ripping Roughsawn
Stock (p. 138)

➤ Ripping Thick
Stock (p. 139)

Advanced Ripping

➤ Using a Short
Fence (p. 140)

➤ Ripping Bevels
(p. 141)

➤ Ripping Live-Edge
Slabs (p. 142)

➤ Resawing in a
Single Pass (p. 143)

➤ Resawing in Two
Passes (p. 144)

**Ripping
Sheet Goods**

➤ Ripping Full-Size
Sheet Stock (p. 145)

➤ Ripping Plastic
Laminate (p. 147)

RIPPING MEANS SAWING PARALLEL to the wood grain. It is most often done when cutting boards to narrower widths, feeding the edge stock against the saw's rip fence. When it comes to ripping, a tablesaw is really in its element. You can rip boards using a bandsaw, a portable circular saw, or other tool; but a tablesaw will do it much more efficiently. It is powerful, and the rip fence allows you to cut identical multiples without having to set up a cutting guide each time, as you would have to with a portable circular saw.

Performed correctly, and with the proper safety accessories, ripping can be done without fear. However, keep in mind that most tablesaw accidents are the result of kickback happening during ripping. That's why it's critical to use a properly aligned splitter every single time you rip.

➤ See "Kickback in Action" on p. 82.

➤ See Section 4.

In this section, I show you how to prepare stock for ripping and how to safely and accurately cut solid lumber as well as sheet stock.

Getting Ready to Rip

Setting up to rip workpieces means mounting the appropriate blade, adjusting the fence, and making sure a splitter is installed (as well as a blade guard when possible). When ripping long stock, you may also want to set up feed support. At first, this may seem like a long litany of preparations just to make a cut, but it all becomes second nature after a bit and goes very quickly.

Selecting a Blade

The blade you use depends on the work you're doing. As discussed in Section 3, you have a lot of blade choices. When I'm doing the preliminary rough sizing of lumber before dressing, I use a 24-tooth ATB rip blade. It cuts fast and saves wear and tear on my premium 40-tooth blade. The rip blade cuts a bit rough, but that doesn't matter because all the workpieces get cut again later when milling them to final size. When ripping lumber or plywood to final size, I typically use my premium 40-tooth blade.

You may find that ripping thick hardwood can bog down a portable saw or contractor's saw. In that case, you may want to use a thin-kerf blade, which moves through the wood easier, although it may not cut quite as smoothly.

It's often recommended that the blade be raised so the bottom of the gullets align with the top of the workpiece. Regardless of the blade used, I typically set the blade height only about $3/8$-in. above the work for safety's

Blade height typically needs to be only $3/8$ in. or so above the workpiece.

sake. Raising it higher will somewhat reduce the backward force on the workpiece but, in my opinion, it's not enough to offset the increased danger posed by a raised blade.

Setting the Fence

Adjust the fence for your desired width of cut, making sure to lock it securely. (If you have switched over to a thin-kerf blade and your fence cursor is normally set for a $1/8$-in. blade, remember to account for the difference.) Safety and quality of cut depend greatly on using a straight fence that's set perfectly parallel to the blade. Some woodworkers cock the end of the fence away from the blade by $1/32$ in. or so, which is fine. What is crucial is that the fence does *not* toe in *toward* the blade. If it does, you're inviting rough cuts, pinching, and burning. Worse yet, if you're working without a splitter, you really increase the danger of kickback.

If you're unfortunate enough to be using an old-style rip fence that protests parallelism to the blade, make doubly sure to measure from the blade to the locked fence at both the front and the rear of the blade.

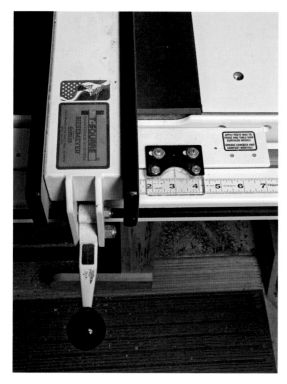

The cursor and scale on a premium rip fence allows quick and accurate setting of the fence.

Even a premium fence goes out of alignment after a while, so make sure to check it occasionally.

For more information see "Fence and Rails" on p. 19.

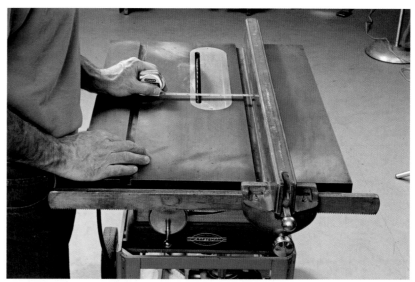

⚠ **WARNING Don't rip without using a properly aligned splitter.**

Kickback and Cut Protection

At the risk of being a nag, let me once again encourage you to use a splitter when ripping. Properly aligned, it will prevent kickback by keeping the workpiece from contacting the rising rear teeth of the blade and being thrown back at you at fierce speeds.

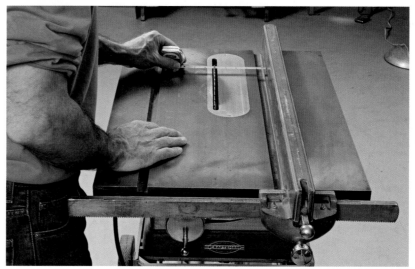

Whatever splitter you use, make sure that it's aligned with the edge of the blade teeth that face the fence. When aligning the splitter, raise the blade as high as possible to create as much distance as you can between the front and the rear teeth.

For more information, see Section 4.

After locking an old-style rip fence like this, make sure to measure to the fence at both the front and the rear of the blade to ensure parallelism.

A properly adjusted splitter aligns with the side of the blade teeth that face the rip fence.

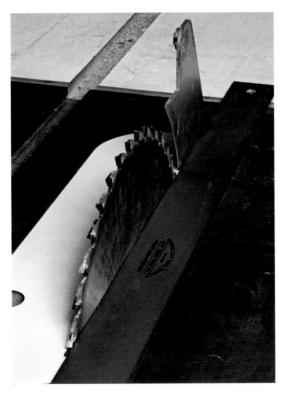

Also, whenever possible, use a blade guard. Not only will it prevent accidental contact with the blade, it will also protect against sawdust being thrown at your face. If you're using an aftermarket overhead guard, make sure its sides aren't too close to the blade.

Feed Support

As far as I'm concerned, an outfeed table is an absolute necessity, even when ripping short pieces. Without one, your work just falls to the floor, possibly damaging sharp edges and corners. Outfeed support is critical when ripping long stock, which may otherwise start to tip off the saw table before the cut is complete, forcing you to put undue pressure on the trailing end of the board right at the spinning blade.

Depending on your skill at feeding long stock, you may also want to set up infeed support, especially for long, heavy boards. This doesn't have to be anything fancy or expensive. It can be as simple as a sure-footed sawhorse with a panel clamped to it.

A plywood panel clamped to a steady sawhorse (above) works fine for infeed support. A bullnose strip on the panel's bearing edge (right) reduces friction.

A router table the same height as the saw serves as great infeed support for floppy, thin materials such as this piece of plastic laminate.

Large sheets of thin stock such as plastic laminate need feed support to keep the material from flopping around. I often use my router table, which I built to match the height of my tablesaw. Instead, you could lay a support sheet of plywood across a couple of sawhorses outfitted with riser panels.

Dress for Success

Last, protect the only eyes and ears you have. Make sure to don safety glasses and hearing protection before you turn on the saw. Although I've met blind woodworkers,

> ## CONFESSIONS OF A REFORMED RIPPER
>
> **Okay, full disclosure here.** Until a few years ago, I was as guilty as any of my woodworking pals when it came to ripping without a splitter. Easily removable/replaceable aftermarket splitters weren't available until fairly recently so, like most woodworkers, I removed my saw's troublesome stock splitter and learned to work without it. But just because I can still count on all 10 of my fingers, I'm not counting myself smart; I'm just counting myself lucky. I've suffered kickback that could have stolen my fingers or bruised me badly. If you want to go out with all the digits you came in with, use a splitter!

none of them would claim any advantage to working in the dark. And I know that my hearing-impaired friends sure miss the sound of music and chirping birds.

Preparing the Stock

To rip wood safely, the edge that contacts the rip fence needs to be straight, and the face that bears against the table should be flat. That way, the board shouldn't pinch against the blade or rock around as you're feeding it. There will be times when you'll have to rip a board with a warped face, but under no circumstances should you ever feed a board with a crooked edge against the fence. A crooked edge can cause a board to either pinch against the side of the blade or to rock sideways during the cut.

Ideally, your stock should be jointed and planed to final thickness before ripping to width. In the process, you create the flat

When ripping, plant yourself firmly with feet splayed in alignment with the blade, and stand to the left of the board.

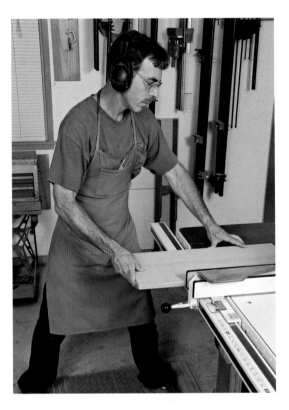

Stance at the Saw

Ripping requires sure-footed balance throughout the process. Here's how it goes: After turning on the saw, lay the board on the table against the fence, with the leading end a couple of inches from the blade. Make certain that the board's leading edge is contacting the table. Otherwise, the blade can slap it down ferociously against the table. Stand slightly to the left of the board, with your splayed legs roughly parallel to the blade and your torso facing the fence. The idea here is to remain solidly grounded and well balanced throughout the cutting process.

Handling and Feeding

Use your left hand to press the board downward and against the fence at the same time.

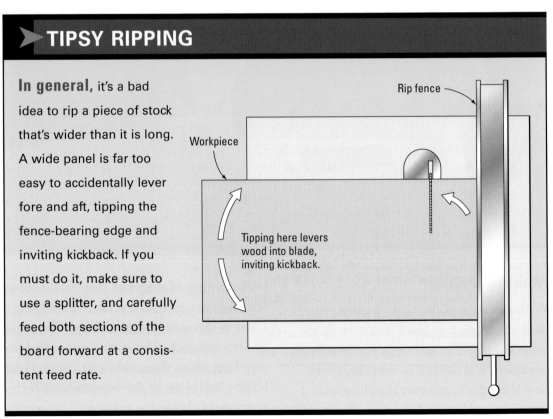

▶ TIPSY RIPPING

In general, it's a bad idea to rip a piece of stock that's wider than it is long. A wide panel is far too easy to accidentally lever fore and aft, tipping the fence-bearing edge and inviting kickback. If you must do it, make sure to use a splitter, and carefully feed both sections of the board forward at a consistent feed rate.

Rip fence

Workpiece

Tipping here levers wood into blade, inviting kickback.

Begin the cut with the board flat on the table and pressed against the fence, with a push stick at the ready (left). When the board is completely on the table, begin pushing with the push stick (center). As the cut nears completion, move your left hand aside and finish up using the push stick (right).

With your right hand on the trailing end, push the board steadily forward into the spinning blade. When the trailing end of the board is completely on the table, pick up your push stick with your right hand and bring it into play while continuing to apply sideways pressure with your left hand forward of the blade. As the cut nears completion, remove your left hand from the board for safety's sake, continuing forward motion with the push stick until the right-hand piece is past the splitter.

Throughout the cut, pay primary attention to the contact of the board against the fence, but do glance at the blade area occasionally to monitor it as well. Feed the board as quickly as you can to prevent burn-

▶ See "Thin-Kerf Blades" on p. 58.

⚠ **WARNING Never reach over a spinning blade to retrieve a workpiece. Either turn the saw off first or walk around to the back of the saw to get it.**

ing. There's no reason to feed slowly unless the saw is bogging down, in which case you should consider using a thin-kerf blade.

Working with a Short Fence

Some rip fences, like the Delta Unifence, allow fore-and-aft adjustment. This type of fence is standard issue on saws in Europe; when ripping on these saws, the far end of the fence is adjusted to extend slightly beyond the point at which the sawteeth enter the work. The idea is that the leading edge of the board is then prevented from pinching between the fence and the rising

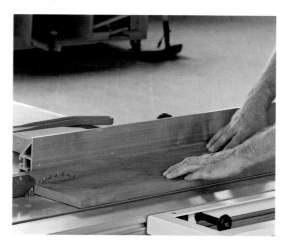

This European saw's rip fence can be retracted so the cut section of the board is never jammed between the blade and the fence.

A BURNING QUESTION

We all know that wood burns, whether from a lit match or from sawblade friction. But how to prevent the latter? Well, you can minimize the problem by avoiding the three primary causes: fence misalignment, a dirty blade, and improper feed speed.

First of all, make sure that your rip fence is adjusted parallel to your blade. If the fence toes inward toward the rear sawteeth, pinching of the board will contribute to burning. Also make sure your blade is clean. Most of us don't clean our blades nearly often enough. Last, make sure to feed your workpiece as quickly and steadily as you can. Pausing or slow feeding are common causes of burning.

▶ See "Cleaning a Blade" on p. 70.

Certain woods, such as cherry, are just burn-prone. No matter how careful you are, you're likely to end up with scorch marks on the edge. The best thing in that case is to rip your finished cut oversize by about 1/32 in., then clean up the edge afterward by taking a single pass on the jointer.

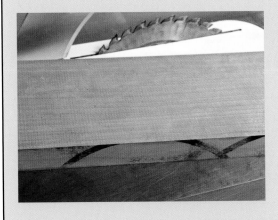

Even when cutting with a clean, well-aligned blade, some woods— like the cherry board shown here—are prone to burning.

Fences that don't adjust fore and aft can be outfitted with an auxiliary short fence that stands off enough to allow a space for rippings to go.

rear teeth of the blade, preventing kickback, jamming, and burning.

A fence setup like this can be particularly helpful if stresses in your workpiece cause it to splay apart as it's cut. If your fence doesn't adjust fore and aft, you can easily outfit it with an auxiliary short fence. Ripping with a short fence might feel a bit odd at first, but you'll get used to it pretty quickly.

▶ See "Using a Short Fence" on p. 140.

Ripping Short Pieces

Ripping pieces from a short length of wood can be dicey because the wood may be nearly cut through before it reaches the splitter, inviting kickback. Therefore, it's usually best to rip a long piece first, and then crosscut it into shorter lengths. However, you may have only short pieces of your chosen wood that need to be ripped down. It is certainly feasible to rip short pieces in the regular fashion—just make sure to use a shoe-style push

When using a shoe-style push stick to rip short pieces, it's important that the sole is straight to maintain maximum contact with the workpiece.

The GRR-Ripper is a highly configurable push block that's ideal for ripping short workpieces.

Pieces can be ripped from short, wide pieces using a crosscut sled.

stick with a straight sole to maintain firm contact along the length of the workpiece. If you like, you can glue a strip of fine sandpaper to the sole to improve friction and help you press the piece sideways against the fence.

If you're ripping a piece from a short, wide board, it's often safer to use a crosscut sled. To ensure that you're not creating tapered pieces, check that the ends of the board are square to its edges. The drawback of using a sled is that making identical mul-

tiples isn't as easy as when feeding against a rip fence because you don't have the immediate registration that the fence offers. If you need to rip short multiples using a sled, you can set up the cuts with a stop block and spacer, as shown later in this section.

► See "Ripping Short Multiples with a Sled" on p. 137

If you work with a lot of small pieces, you may want to invest in a GRR-Ripper or two. This tool is a highly configurable push block with a nonskid bottom, an adjustable center leg to keep the offcut from straying after the cut, and an outer stabilizing leg that can be adjusted up or down to create solid, level footing on the workpiece and saw table. In my experience, it's the quickest, safest way to rip small pieces of all sorts.

► For buying information, see "Resources" on p. 217.

Feeding stock against an L-shaped auxiliary fence gives you more room to maneuver your push stick when ripping narrow pieces.

Grinding off the pawl mounting hub on an aftermarket splitter allows passage of a push stick when ripping narrow pieces.

Ripping Narrow Pieces

Many project parts call for very narrow pieces, such as runners for small drawers, decorative trim, and strips to cover the raw edges of plywood. Sawing narrow pieces presents a challenge because of their size. I find that a blade guard tends to impede the use of a push stick when ripping anything narrower than about 1 in. To gain some maneuvering room, you can attach an L-shaped auxiliary fence to your rip fence, as shown in the top left photo above. However, this still won't help when ripping very narrow stock because the side of the guard would be dangerously close to the blade.

If you have only a piece or two to cut, you can safely saw them from the outer edge of a board rather than from the edge that meets the fence. However, this requires resetting the rip fence for each cut and is very inefficient if you want to rip a bunch of pieces to the same size. So what to do when you need to cut a lot of, say, $1/4$-in.-wide strips for plywood edging? Well, I won't kid you, this is one operation I don't use a guard for, although I certainly use a splitter to prevent kickback. If your splitter includes barbed pawls, however, you'll find that they get in the way of a push stick too.

I find pawls more of an impediment than a help (European-style riving knives certainly don't include them), so I removed mine and ground off the mounting hub on the fence-side of my splitter. If you don't want to remove yours, use a short splitter that installs in your zero-clearance throat plate.

▶ See ""Throat Plate-Mounted Splitters" on p. 76.

Other than that, it's not particularly tricky to rip narrow pieces. Just make sure to use a zero-clearance throat plate, and a push stick that's a bit narrower than the finished pieces. Keep the push stick tight against the fence, and hold it down firmly throughout the cut.

[TIP] When cutting narrow strips for plywood edging, rip them $1/16$ in. oversize, then plane $1/32$ in. from each side to clean up the cuts while bringing the pieces down to final size.

When ripping narrow pieces, make sure to keep the push stick snug against the fence while pushing down firmly on the stock.

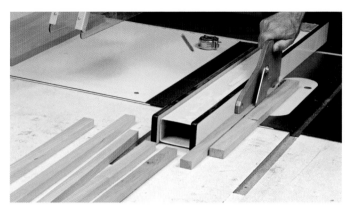

The tablesaw is ideally suited to ripping multiple pieces of identical width.

Ripping Multiples

A lot of woodworking chores involve ripping multiple pieces to identical widths, whether for frames, cabinet parts, doors, box sides, or whatever. Because of its rip fence, the tablesaw excels at this job more than any other tool. You can set the fence once, then shove all sorts of boards through the saw, confident that the resulting pieces will all match in width.

When ripping multiples, it's often a good idea to first joint any edge that will ride against the rip fence. You could just feed the previously sawn edge against the fence, but jointing it first will straighten the edge and correct any slight warping caused by stresses relieved from the previous cut. It also yields a smoother edge than you'll get from most sawblades. Once you get the sawing/jointing system down, as explained later in this section, it goes pretty quickly.

▶ See "Ripping Multiples" on p. 136.

Ripping a Bevel

When ripping bevels, it's important to orient the workpiece properly to ensure a clean-cut, burn-free sawn surface. You want the beveled edge of the keeper piece to be above the tilted blade, as shown in the drawing on p. 130. Otherwise, it would be trapped between the blade and the fence, inviting burning or rough cutting if a bow in the board causes it to lift up against the blade.

[TIP] To ensure a consistent bevel, work with stock that has been dressed flat, square, and with parallel edges.

With a right-tilt saw, this generally means you'll have to work with the rip fence to the left of the blade. This may feel a bit awkward at first, but you'll quickly get used to it. The real problem with beveling on a right-tilt saw is that the fence typically has only about 12 in. of travel to the left of the blade. Therefore, beveling very wide panels forces you to work with the fence to the right, trapping the bevel under the blade. In this case, just do your best to keep the panel pressed down firmly against the saw table near the blade to prevent it from lifting.

RIPPING BEVELS

Preferred

Left-tilt saw with fence to right of blade or right-tilt saw with fence to left of blade (as viewed from rear of saw).

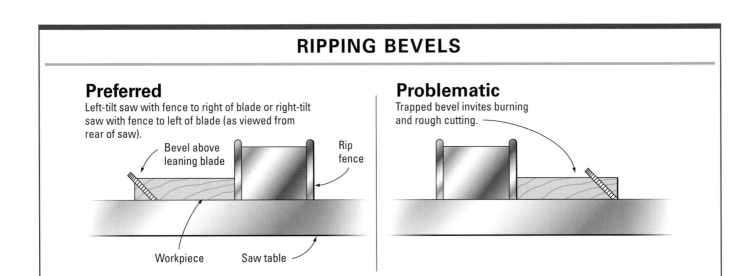

Bevel above leaning blade

Rip fence

Workpiece

Saw table

Problematic

Trapped bevel invites burning and rough cutting.

Ripping bevels on a right-tilt saw requires working with the fence to the left of the blade to avoid trapping the finished bevel under the blade.

To rip a straight edge on a slab of waney lumber, tack a guide board to the piece for safe feeding against the rip fence.

Ripping Live-Edge Stock

Slabbed lumber often has untrimmed, waney edges, sometimes called "live" edges. Ripping a live-edge slab requires first creating one straight edge that can then be safely fed against the rip fence to make subsequent rip cuts. Making the first cut is a simple matter of temporarily tacking a straightedge guide board to the slab. I keep several 6-in.-wide lengths of 1/4-in.-thick plywood on hand for this, using whichever one most closely matches the length of slab to be cut.

Resawing

The technique of resawing means slicing wood across its widest dimension. Really a form of slabbing, it's done to convert thick stock into thin stock and to create book-

After resawing this spalted sycamore board, the two halves are opened like a book to reveal a nearly symmetrical figure.

matched figure. To book-match, the piece is resawn, then the two halves are "opened" as you would a book, creating a nearly symmetrical figure. The two pieces can then be edge-joined to make a book-matched board for use as a door panel, box lid, or other item.

Resawing is usually associated with the bandsaw, and for good reason. A bandsaw is more capable than a tablesaw of resawing wider boards in one pass. Plus, the thin blade on a bandsaw makes a considerably narrower kerf, reducing waste and increasing the number of slices obtainable from a given board. Having said that, it's also true that resawing neatly on a bandsaw can be fussy and depends on a sharp blade, well-adjusted guides, and a meticulous fence setup.

RIPPING STEEP BEVELS

It can be tough to rip a neat, knife-edge bevel that's more acute than 45 degrees. Because a tablesaw blade won't tilt more than 45 degrees, the workpiece can't be laid flat on the saw table to make the cut. Ripping such an acute angle requires feeding the workpiece vertically against the rip fence. Unfortunately, this makes for a somewhat dicey operation; and because the board exits the blade traveling on the knife edge, it's subject to damage.

In a case like this, I use a thick, squared-up carrier board to do the job safely and securely. Wide workpieces can be clamped to the carrier board, but I prefer the less cumbersome approach of making the workpiece a bit oversize in length, then screwing it to the carrier board at both ends. I cut away the screw holes later.

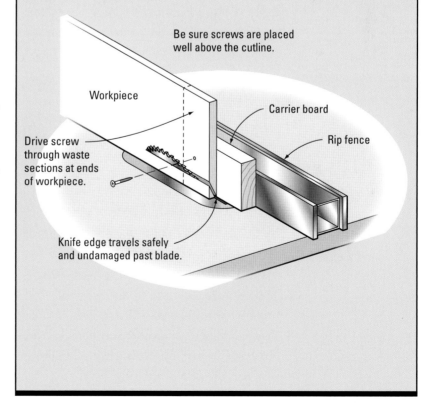

Be sure screws are placed well above the cutline.

Workpiece

Carrier board

Rip fence

Drive screw through waste sections at ends of workpiece.

Knife edge travels safely and undamaged past blade.

Resawing on the tablesaw involves deep cutting, which is aided by featherboards and other hold-downs.

In a sense, resawing on the tablesaw is really nothing more than ripping very thick stock. However, making such a deep cut, especially with the stock on edge, can feel like a somewhat dicey operation. With the proper saw setup, though, it can be done fairly safely. To maximize the resawing capabilities of your saw, you can cut in from both edges of a board to effectively double the cutting depth of the blade.

▶ See "Resawing in Two Passes" on p. 144.

Sheet Stock

Making cabinetry and furniture often involves sawing plywood, hardboard, MDF, plastic laminate, and other sheet stock. The challenge in working with sheet stock lies in its size. Full-size sheets are typically 4 ft. by 8 ft., and larger sizes are available. You can often purchase 4-ft. by 4-ft. "half-sheets" or other smaller panels from your local home supply center, but usually at premium prices. It's most economical to buy full-size sheets and cut them up yourself.

Panel Feed Support

The best kind of tablesaw for handling full-size sheet goods is a "panel saw" with a sliding table. Once the sheet is laid on the sliding table, it's an easy matter to simply push the table forward. However, the work can also be done easily enough on a typical tablesaw using the right approach and setup.

▶ See "Panel Saws" on p. 12.

First of all, you need proper feed support. This is where a large outfeed table will serve you well. It's best if the table extends at least 50 in. beyond the splitter so an 8-ft.-long sheet won't tip at the end of the cut. You may also want to set up infeed support for heavier panels. It's rare that you'll need side support when ripping, as long as you plan out a sensible cut sequence.

Rip Sequence

Planning the proper cut sequence can save you untold aggravation. Begin by ripping the sheet into easily maneuverable pieces, keeping in mind that you'll ultimately want to cut away any factory edges in the process. As an example, let's take a look at how we might cut a full-size sheet into case parts for a 24-in.-wide base cabinet and wall cabinet, both of standard depth.

An outfeed table that extends 50 in. past the saw splitter will prevent a standard 8-ft.-long panel from tipping after the cut.

The drawing at right shows one economical layout. The first cut would be a full length rip down the center of the panel. If you feed carefully, this will be a clean, finished cut. Next, saw the wall cabinet sections from the two halves you just cut (cuts 2 and 3). Leave them slightly oversize in length so the short factory edges can be trimmed away later. Set your rip fence for the base cabinet width. Feed the previously ripped edge (cut 1) against the fence, ripping the pieces to final width as you trim away the factory edge (cuts 4 and 5). Set the fence for the wall cabinet width and rip those pieces in the same manner (cuts 6 through 9). All that's left is to crosscut the pieces to length, as discussed in Section 8.

A CASE STUDY IN PANEL LAYOUT

This 4-in. by 8-in. plywood sheet is economically laid out to yield parts for a standard base cabinet and wall cabinet. Ripping the parts in the sequence shown makes for easy handling and removal of factory edges.

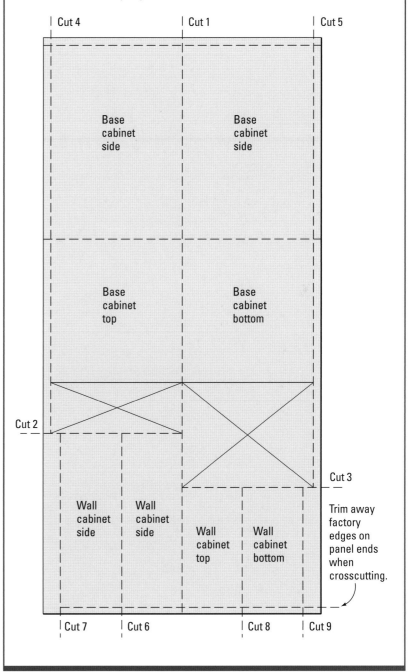

A FENCE JIG FOR RIPPING THIN SHEET STOCK

This simple fence jig will make ripping thin sheet stock like plastic laminate a breeze. A strip of ¼-in.-thick plywood glued to the underside of an MDF or plywood auxiliary fence prevents thin material from being trapped by any gap under your tablesaw fence. It also raises the sheet just enough to accommodate the heel of a push stick. A hold-down strip clamped above the workpiece keeps it from riding up on the fence. Make the hold-down 3 in. to 4 in. shorter than the auxiliary fence to allow inspection of workpiece/fence contact at both ends of the fence.

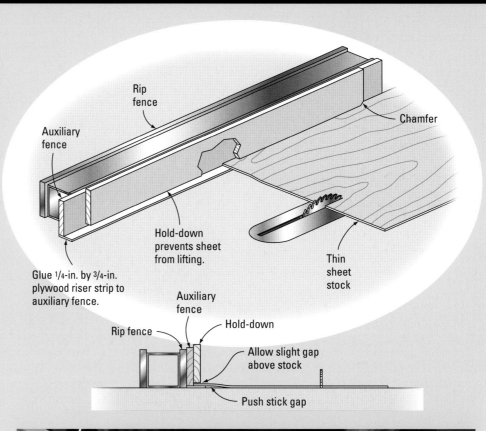

Rip fence

Chamfer

Auxiliary fence

Hold-down prevents sheet from lifting.

Thin sheet stock

Glue ¼-in. by ¾-in. plywood riser strip to auxiliary fence.

Auxiliary fence

Rip fence

Hold-down

Allow slight gap above stock

Push stick gap

Ripping Long Stock

Ripping long stock can be cumbersome and inaccurate if you're not properly set up. Most important, you need good infeed and outfeed support. A strong light directed at your rip fence is very helpful for monitoring fence contact when you're positioned at some distance from the saw.

▶ See "Feed Support" on p. 120.

Set your rip fence for the desired width of cut, then position your infeed support so it will support the board as much as possible while leaving clear passage for your feed hand **(A)**. Raise the blade and position the board against the rip fence 1 in. or so in front of the blade. With your feet planted widely, grasp the end of the board with your right hand, and extend your left hand as far forward as is comfortably possible **(B)**. If necessary to ensure good board contact against the fence, rock the board side to side a bit, letting it rest solidly against the fence.

> ⚠ **WARNING A helper who is supporting boards should never attempt to grab or steer the stock but simply support it with palms facing upward.**

Turn on the saw and feed the board forward, keeping your undivided attention on the fence **(C)**. Push the board steadily, applying pressure against the fence with your left hand as soon as it reaches the table area **(D)**. When the trailing end of the board is on the table, transfer the pushing force of your right hand to the end of the board. Remove your left hand from the board before it gets closer than about 8 in. from the blade **(E)**. (A wide board like this allows safe passage for your right hand, but use a push stick for anything narrower than about 10 in.) Complete the cut, and follow through by pushing the keeper piece just past the splitter **(F)**.

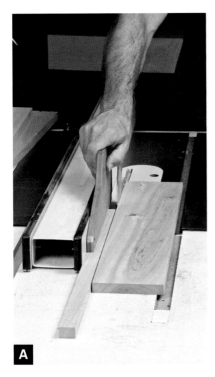

A

B

C

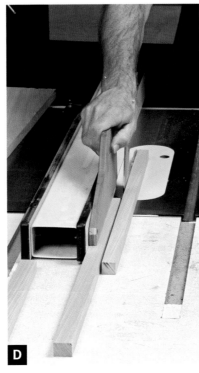

D

Ripping Multiples

There's nothing tricky about ripping multiples, and there are certain efficiencies to be gained in the process. Develop a system that suits your aims. For example, it's quickest to simply rip pieces in sequence from a board or boards, but you'll end up with a lot of pieces that have two sawn edges. Depending on what you'll be using the pieces for, the edges may then have to be cleaned up on a jointer or with a handplane. Unfortunately, jointing opposing edges of a board can create edges that are out of parallel. I'll discuss an approach here that results in pieces of identical width with clean, parallel edges.

Working with thicknessed stock, begin by jointing one edge of each blank to be ripped. For efficiency, stack the blanks to the right of the fence with the jointed edge to the right. Set the rip fence for the desired width of cut plus $1/32$ in. With the jointed edge against the fence, rip your first piece **(A)**. At the end of the cut, push the ripped piece as far past the blade as you comfortably can **(B)**. Step around to the side of the saw and push the piece out of the cut path **(C)**. Set the remainder of the blank aside for now, and rip a piece from the next blank, whose edge you have already jointed **(D)**. When you have ripped a piece from each of your boards, take the blanks to the jointer and clean up the sawn edge in preparation for the next cut. Repeat until done.

Ripping Short Multiples with a Sled

You can cut identical multiples on a sled using a stop block and spacer. This prevents trapping the cutoff between the blade and a stop block at the end of the cut, which is always a no-no.

Begin by placing your workpiece in position for the desired rip cut, and butt a short piece against it to serve as a spacer **(A)**. Butt a stop block against the spacer and clamp it to the sled fence **(B)**. Keeping the workpiece in position, remove the spacer and make the cut **(C)**. Pull the sled back away from the blade before taking away the newly cut piece **(D)**. Repeat each subsequent rip in the same manner.

As the workpiece gets narrower, keep it perpendicular to the fence by placing a squared panel against its left-hand edge. Use a panel that is the same thickness as the workpiece so that it also serves as a riser to help support a thick hold-down block **(E)**.

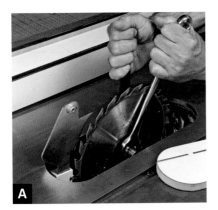

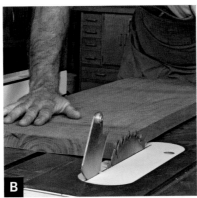

Ripping Roughsawn Stock

Many cabinetmakers and furniture builders begin their projects with roughsawn stock. After cutting the raw boards roughly to length, the next step is often ripping the pieces roughly to width. To start this process you'll need to create a straight edge to bear against the fence. After that, the challenge is ripping pieces that may have slightly cupped faces that rock a bit on the saw table. (*Note:* Severely cupped boards should be ripped with a bandsaw or jigsaw.)

▶ **See "Preparing the Stock" on p. 121.**

Orienting the concave face downward provides more solid footing but invites collapse at the end of the cut, pinching the keeper piece between the blade and the fence and inviting kickback if you're not using a splitter. If a splitter is installed, the collapsed board can jam against it, impeding feed. I prefer to feed a cupped board convex side down, firmly pressing down the edge nearest the fence, which prevents collapse at the end of the cut.

Mount a 24-tooth rip blade on your saw **(A)**. The rough surface it leaves won't matter at this point. Set the blade height, making sure it will extend about 3/8 in. above the high edge of the board when pressed down at the opposite edge **(B)**.

Set the fence for the desired width of cut, make sure to install a splitter, and have a push stick at the ready. Begin feeding the board, firmly holding down the edge of the board nearest the fence **(C)**. As soon as the trailing end of the board is on the saw table, bring your push stick into play **(D)**. Follow through to the end of the cut using the push stick, and the offcut will fall harmlessly to the table **(E)**.

Ripping Thick Stock

There's nothing particularly difficult about ripping thick stock, except that you're sawing through a lot of wood in one pass, which can stress an underpowered saw. As always, begin by thicknessing the stock and jointing one edge straight and square for safe travel along the fence. It's generally best to mount a 24-tooth rip blade on your saw **(A)**. Set your rip fence for the desired width of cut plus $1/32$ in. (which you'll remove later on the jointer to clean up the rough rip cut). Raise the blade about $3/8$ in. above the workpiece, make sure a splitter is installed, and place a push stick at the ready **(B)**.

Turn on the saw, and place the board on the table against the rip fence, keeping it safely away from the front of the blade. Apply sideways and downward pressure with your left hand, placing your right hand or push stick on the trailing end **(C)**. (This board is short enough that it lays almost entirely on the table, so the push stick can be brought into play from the start.) Feed the board steadily and surely into the blade, pushing as quickly as you comfortably can without bogging down the saw. Continue to apply sideways pressure against the fence, but never let your left hand move past the front of the insert plate **(D)**. Once the board passes your left hand, continue feeding with only the push stick **(E)**. After the blade has separated the pieces, follow through with the push stick until the workpiece is past the splitter **(F)**.

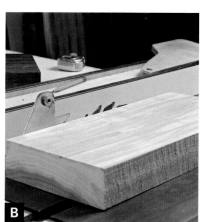

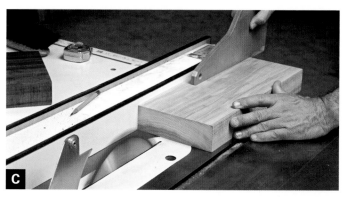

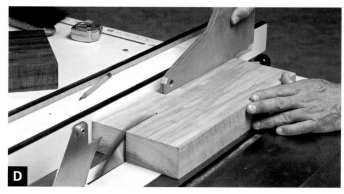

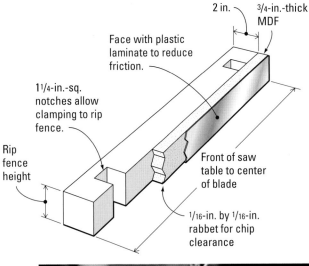

2 in.

3/4-in.-thick MDF

Face with plastic laminate to reduce friction.

1¼-in.-sq. notches allow clamping to rip fence.

Rip fence height

Front of saw table to center of blade

1/16-in. by 1/16-in. rabbet for chip clearance

Using a Short Fence

Begin by setting the blade height. With the stock placed next to the blade, note the point at which the teeth will enter the stock. Then locate the leading end of the short fence 1 in. or 2 in. past that point, and clamp it in place **(A)**. With a push stick at hand, place the workpiece solidly on the saw table, and press it sideways against the fence using your left hand **(B)**. Maintaining downward and sideways pressure, feed the board into the blade at a steady, brisk rate. As soon as the trailing edge of the board is on the saw table, hold it securely with your left hand as you quickly pick up your push stick and continue feeding with your right **(C)**. When the piece separates at the end of the cut, continue to push straight forward **(D)**. If the piece veers a bit toward the open space near the fence, that's okay. It's that little bit of freedom at the end of the cut that takes some getting used to.

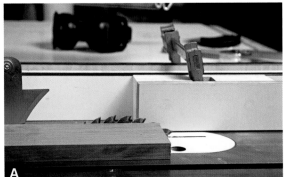

A

B

C

D

Ripping Bevels

To rip bevels, make sure your saw is outfitted with its stock throat plate, whose opening is wide enough to allow the blade to tilt. It's best to use a splitter to prevent kickback, but I realize that you may have only a shopmade splitter, which won't tilt with the blade. If you're forced to work without a splitter, take great care to hold the workpiece against the fence to prevent it from drifting toward the blade.

Raise the blade and crank it over to the desired angle. Mark the cutline on the end of the workpiece and adjust the fence to set up the cut **(A)**. Take a nip cut to make sure you're on your line **(B)**. After making any necessary fence adjustment, begin the rip, holding the piece firmly against the fence **(C)**. As soon as the piece is entirely on the saw table, bring your push stick into play **(D)**. Follow through with the push stick until the cut is complete **(E)**.

A

B

C

D

E

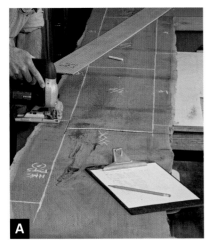

A

B

C

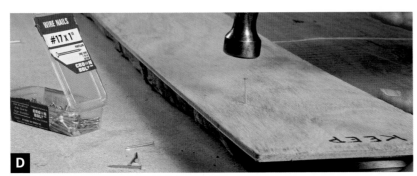

D

E

Ripping Live-Edge Slabs

Begin by laying out your parts on the slab using chalk. Mark the parts at least ¼ in. oversize in width and 1 in. or 2 in. oversize in length. It's more efficient if you can start off with a single straight rip along the full length of a slab. However, if the slab is particularly long, you may want to crosscut it into more manageable pieces (no longer than 8 ft. or so), Use a jigsaw to make these crosscuts as it will allow you to jog the cuts as necessary **(A)**.

Place a plywood straightedge on the slab and slide it over until the entire slab edge just peeks out from under it. (The idea here is to maximize the plywood's bearing on the slab **(B)**. Then position the straightedge parallel to your cutline, keeping its overhang on the slab to a minimum **(C)**. Using 1-in. nails, tack the plywood to the slab in two or three places, leaving the nail heads a bit proud for removal afterward **(D)**. Drive the nails in near the ends and edge, which will be sawn away later.

Measure from the outside edge of the straightedge to the cutline **(E)**, and set your rip fence for this measurement. Make the cut, keeping the straightedge against the fence as you go **(F)**.

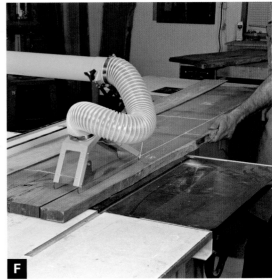

F

Resawing in a Single Pass

When resawing a board into thinner boards, the first order of business is to joint and plane the piece to consistent thickness, then joint the edges square to the faces. A consistent thickness ensures that the piece rides accurately against the rip fence, that the piece won't lean during the cut, and that a featherboard will maintain constant pressure.

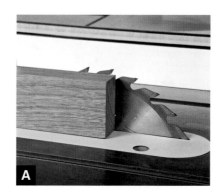
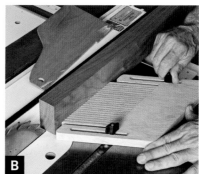

When resawing, you'll generally want to mount a 24-tooth resaw blade on your saw because it will move through the stock easily. The cut will be a bit rough, but you'll clean up the face later anyway. However, when resawing pine or other soft stock, a premium-quality 40-tooth blade can give you a cut that needs almost no cleanup at all, providing your saw is tuned well and the blade is clean and sharp, preventing burning.

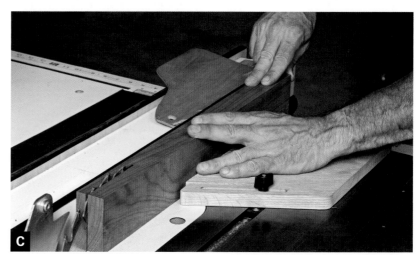

When resawing in a single pass, install a splitter, and set your blade height to be no more than about ¼ in. above the stock **(A)**. Adjust your rip fence for the desired thickness of the piece plus ¹⁄₃₂ in., which will be planed away later. For best safety and accuracy, set up a featherboard to press against the stock just in front of the blade **(B)**. Also place a push stick at hand.

Begin the cut, holding the piece down with your left hand and pushing it forward with your right **(C)**. Feed at a steady rate as fast as you comfortably can. As soon as the trailing end of the board is resting on the table, bring your push stick into play **(D)**. Follow through, using the push stick until the cut is completed **(E)**. Before beginning the next cut, joint the face that will be contacting the fence. Then repeat the process as before.

A

B

C

D

E

F

Resawing in Two Passes

Resawing can be done in two passes instead of one, making for a safer operation because each of the two cuts is shallower than a full cut (on all but the widest pieces). Resawing in two passes also allows you to slice a wider board, as shown here. Prepare the stock and install a blade.

▶ See "Resawing in a Single Pass" on p. 143.

Although a typical splitter won't work for this non-through cut, you can use a short splitter mounted in a zero-clearance throat plate. When resawing wide pieces, use a tall fence. This may be as simple as an auxiliary fence screwed to your rip fence, or you can make a box-style fence.

▶ See "Splitters" on p. 73.

▶ See "Auxiliary Tall Fence" on p. 47.

Set the fence for the desired finished thickness plus $\frac{1}{32}$ in. (You'll plane away the extra bit afterward **(A)**.) Raise the blade to reach about halfway through the stock, and set up a featherboard **(B)**.

Feed the board steadily and as quickly as you comfortably can. The splitter will hold the cut half safely against the fence **(C)**. Complete this first cut, continuing to hold the piece firmly against the tall fence **(D)**.

Flip the piece end for end, with the same face against the fence. Place a push stick at the ready, then begin the cut in the same manner as before **(E)**. For safety's sake, use a push stick to complete the cut, as the two parts will separate entirely once past the blade **(F)**. Before resawing the next slice, joint the face that will be contacting the fence. Then repeat the entire process as required.

Ripping Full-Size Sheet Stock

Ripping 4-ft. by 8-ft. sheets of plywood, MDF, or other sheet stock isn't difficult if you set up properly for the cut. For easiest handling, begin with whichever cut is closest to the center of the panel. In this case, I'll be ripping right down the center of the panel, which is not an uncommon cut when making typical cabinet parts.

Set up infeed support and lock your rip fence in position for the desired width. Rather than trying to hoist the panel onto the saw and infeed support, I find that it's easiest to first place the panel on the saw (with the blade lowered and the splitter removed), then drag it onto the infeed support. (I'm using my router table here for support **(A)**. With your splitter reinstalled, adjust the blade height using a piece of scrap plywood **(B)**. Place the leading edge of the panel against the fence just 1 in. or so in front of the blade. You want as much of the edge against the fence as possible without hitting the blade.

[TIP] To help monitor fence contact from a distance, train a strong overhead light on the side of the fence where it meets the workpiece.

Turn the saw on and position yourself at the corner of the panel, with your right hand grasping the trailing edge and your left hand as far forward on the outside edge as is comfortably possible **(C)**. Maintain a wide stance for strength and balance. Keeping your eyes glued to the fence (using "contact lens cement"), push the panel straight forward with your right hand, and apply enough sideways pressure with your left hand to keep the panel against the fence **(D)**. Keep pushing in this fashion until the saw is carrying the full

(text continues on p. 146.)

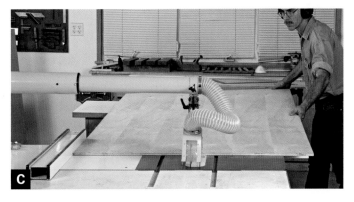

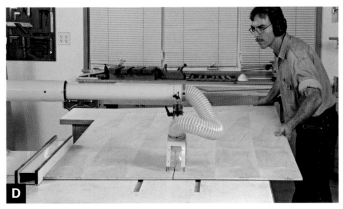

weight of the sheet **(E)**. Let the panel sit for just a moment, and move around to its rear edge and place your hands so that each one is centered between the blade and the panel edge **(F)**. All the while, maintain your focus on the fence. Continue pushing straight forward with each hand until the cut is complete **(G)**.

[VARIATION] **If you find it difficult to keep the panel against the fence at the beginning of the cut, you can clamp on a thick fence extension to provide increased bearing. It needs to extend only 1 in. or so past the front of the blade.**

VARIATION

Ripping Plastic Laminate

Thin stock such as plastic laminate tends to slip into the gap under the rip fence. It also tries to ride on top of the spinning blade if the sheet isn't held down. You can solve both of these problems by using a simple shopmade jig. The two-piece jig consists of an L-shaped auxiliary fence and a hold-down strip. The auxiliary fence attaches to your rip fence, and the hold-down attaches to the auxiliary fence.

▶ See "A Fence Jig for Ripping Thin Sheet Stock" on p. 134.

Rather than clamping the jig to the fence, which can interfere with my push stick, I attach the parts with thin double-faced tape **(A)**. For a good bond, apply clamp pressure to the taped areas for a few moments **(B)**. Place the workpiece against the auxiliary fence with some scraps of plastic laminate on top to allow for clearance. Attach the hold-down **(C)**, centering it on the auxiliary fence for visibility at both ends.

With the blade raised about ⅜ in. above the stock, set up your fence, working to a cutline on your stock instead of your fence's cursor. Use a splitter to keep the stock safely against the fence, and have your push stick at the ready. To make the cut, tuck the workpiece under the hold-down and against the fence. As you feed the stock with your right hand, use your left hand to hold down the piece in front of the blade, never letting your hand get too close to the blade **(D)**. When the laminate's trailing edge is completely on the table, employ your push stick, running it along the face of the hold-down with its heel hooked on the edge of the laminate **(E)**. Push the keeper piece past the splitter, having taken your left hand out of play **(F)**.

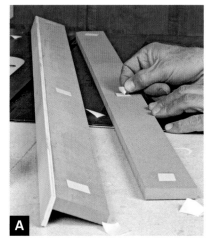

A

B

C

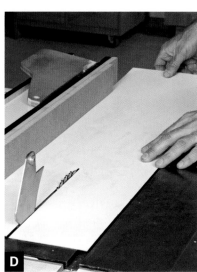

D

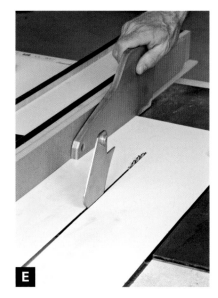

E

F

Crosscutting

Basic Crosscutting

➤ Simple Crosscut with a Miter Gauge (p. 158)

➤ Simple Crosscut with a Sled (p. 159)

Specialty Crosscutting

➤ Beveling on a Sled (p. 160)

Cutting Multiples

➤ Multiples with a Stop Block (p. 161)

➤ Multiples with a Flip Stop (p. 162)

➤ Multiples with a Fence Block (p. 163)

➤ Multiples with a Sled (p. 164)

CROSSCUTTING MEANS SAWING perpendicular to the grain of a workpiece. It is most often performed when cutting workpieces to length but also comes into play when cutting joints and certain shapes. For example, the shoulder of a tenon is made with a shallow crosscut. Also, a miter is an angled crosscut used to create frame corners and other constructions. When crosscutting, a workpiece is fed into the blade guided by a miter gauge, a crosscut sled, or the fence on a sliding table. In this section, I show you how to crosscut accurately, efficiently, and cleanly to help ensure your work looks good and your joints go together properly.

➤ For more on cutting tenons and miters, see Section 10.

Crucial Crosscutting Accessories

For crosscutting, you need an accurate, nononsense method of carrying the workpiece past the blade. Your options include a miter gauge, a crosscut sled, and a sliding table. A miter gauge is generally fine for relatively small workpieces, but it's not big enough to handle large boards and panels. For these, turn to a crosscut sled which, depending on its size, can provide enough capacity for

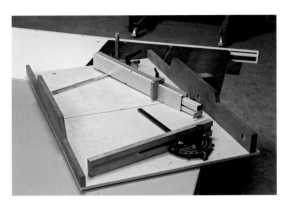

Crosscutting on the tablesaw can be done with a miter gauge or a crosscut sled.

DON'T WORK UNDRESSED

Crosscutting is usually the last step in "dressing" a workpiece to final size. As discussed in Section 11, a workpiece should first be jointed, thicknessed, and ripped to width before being crosscut to length. If stock isn't milled in the proper order, the crosscut ends may not end up square. Plus, the edge of the workpiece needs to be dead straight so it bears solidly against the miter gauge or sled fence when crosscutting.

▶ See "Dressing Roughsawn Stock" on p. 209.

feeding all but the largest panels. In many ways, the best overall crosscutting solution is a large integral sliding table. Unfortunately, relatively few tablesaws in North America are equipped with them, and they tend to be somewhat expensive.

Because I've discussed all of these tools at length in Sections 1 and 2, I devote this section to using them. I don't have a sliding table on my saw, so I'll be doing the work with miter gauges and crosscut sleds.

Preparing to Crosscut

Before crosscutting, a few things need to be in order: The proper blade needs to be installed as well as a splitter and guard if possible. If you're using a miter gauge instead of a sled, its angle needs to be set accurately.

As discussed in Section 3, you can use a 60- or 80-tooth blade specifically designed for crosscutting, but a premium-quality 40- or 50-tooth blade can do the job satisfactorily. When doing a lot of back-and-forth ripping and crosscutting, I normally crosscut with my 40-tooth blade, switching over the 80-tooth only when doing a dedicated run of concerted crosscutting.

The premium-quality, all-purpose 40-tooth blade at left cuts nearly as well as the 80-tooth blade at right, with only a bit more exit tearout on the underside.

Set the blade height about 3/8 in. above the height of the workpiece. Make sure the blade angle is set at exactly 90 degrees by making a test cut and gauging it with an accurate square. For the cleanest cuts, outfit your saw with a zero-clearance insert plate, which will also prevent thin offcut slices from falling into your saw.

▶ See "Making a Zero-Clearance Throat Plate" on p. 38.

A zero-clearance insert plate backs up the wood fibers adjacent to the cut, minimizing exit tearout.

An overhead guard can be used with a miter gauge by sliding the gauge's fence to the side of the guard.

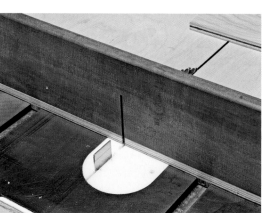

A low-profile splitter installed in a zero-clearance insert plate can be used with a crosscut sled.

Use a splitter for crosscutting whenever possible because it can keep an offcut from errantly clipping the blade and zinging you. A crosscut sled won't allow the use of a tall stock splitter, but you can use a shopmade wood or aluminum splitter installed in a zero-clearance insert plate.

Use a blade guard whenever possible. Unfortunately, the fence on a crosscut sled will impede a guard, but a miter gauge fence can be adjusted to the side and out of the guard's path. And, as with all tablesaw operations, don't forget to don your safety glasses and hearing protectors.

> ▶ See "Throat Plate–Mounted Splitters" on p. 76.

Basic Crosscutting Procedure

Crosscuts can be made a variety of ways, depending on the size of the workpiece and what is guiding it. However, the basic procedure is the same.

Use a sharp pencil to mark your cutline across the face and down the leading edge of the stock. Place the work firmly against your miter gauge or sled fence; and, with the saw off, align the edge of a sawtooth with the cutline. If your miter gauge fence abuts the blade exactly, you can simply line up the cutline with the end of the fence. Alternatively,

► UNGUARDED EXCUSES

You may wonder why I don't have some sort of guard on my crosscut sled. It certainly is possible to outfit a sled with a removable or permanent shop-made guard. A removable guard often takes the form of a clear polycarbonate "tunnel" guided by slots or cleats in the sled's fences. It's placed atop the work on the sled after the cut has been set up, then is removed afterward. Permanent guards take a variety of forms—the simplest being a polycarbonate shield screwed to the fences over the blade slot.

Perhaps it's a poor excuse, but the reason I don't use a removable guard is efficiency. I'm generally making a lot of crosscuts in a session, and constantly resetting a guard slows me down. As for permanent guards, they require sliding the stock in from the end of the sled. While that's fine for a lot of pieces, my narrow shop won't allow that with long boards. In any case, you can bet that I'm extremely careful where I position my hands when using a sled.

Sandor Nagyszalanczy's crosscut sled includes a blade guard that can be slipped in place atop the workpiece to be cut.

When cross cutting, hold the stock firmly against the fence while pushing the miter gauge forward at a consistent speed.

A cutline laid out across the leading edge of the stock serves as setup reference. A line across the upper face allows monitoring the entire cut.

If an offcut is long enough, you can safely knock it aside using a push stick instead of having to shut the saw down between each cut to clear the table.

A long auxiliary fence that extends past the blade offers a kerf for cut alignment and pushes small offcuts past the blade for safer removal.

CARDINAL CROSSCUTTING SINS

For safety and accuracy, avoid the following mistakes:

- Never slice so little from the end of a board that you don't create an offcut. Nipping off just a tad from an end can cause the blade to deflect, resulting in a nonsquare cut.

- Never hold the offcut section of a piece being sawn. It can cause the cut to pinch. Let it fall away by itself.

- Never crosscut using the rip fence itself as a stop block. The freed offcut can pinch and jam between the fence and blade, causing kickback.

if your miter gauge fence extends past the blade, you can align the cutline with the saw kerf in the fence.

[TIP] A miter gauge can be used in either table slot, but the majority of right-handed woodworkers find it most comfortable to use the left-hand slot.

Standing behind the "keeper" piece, turn on the saw and let it reach full speed. Push the piece slowly forward into the blade, increasing the feed speed as soon as you make contact. With one hand, hold the

workpiece against the fence, pushing the miter gauge with the other. Proper feed speed will depend on the thickness and density of the wood. In general, feed more slowly than when ripping. The important thing is to feed at a consistent speed.

When the cut is complete, slide the keeper piece a bit away from the blade before retracting the miter gauge or sled to prevent grazing the blade on the return stroke. If the offcut is long enough, you can remove it safely by hand or knock it away from the blade with a push stick. With small pieces, you may have to shut off the saw first. If a small trimming gets wedged in the gap beside the blade, always turn off the saw before removing it. Do not keep working and expect the next cut to shove it out of the way.

Stop Blocks and Flip Stops

When cutting multiple workpieces to the same length, it's best to register the end of each piece against a stop to make the cut. It's much more efficient than marking a cutline on each piece, and you can be sure that all of the pieces will be exactly the same length.

Crosscutting a piece almost always involves making two cuts—one at each end. A stop block is used only for the second cut. If you have a number of pieces to cut to the same length, first slice one end square on every piece, then set up a stop for cutting the other end.

Flip stops offer an even better approach because you can perform a quick two-step cut sequence instead of handling each workpiece twice. First, with the flip stop raised up out of the way, make the initial cut to square up one end. Then flip the stop down,

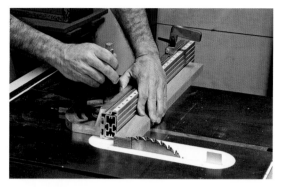

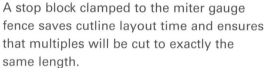

A stop block clamped to the miter gauge fence saves cutline layout time and ensures that multiples will be cut to exactly the same length.

butt the cut end against it, and make your second cut to final length. You can even set up two or more flip stops on a fence for cutting pieces of different lengths, leaving them locked in place should you need to make a replacement piece later.

When using a flip stop, first square up one end of the piece with the stop raised up out of the way. Then flip it down to serve as a stop for cutting the piece to final length.

Short Pieces

Working with short pieces is challenging. When cutting jewelry box drawer pulls or other little parts from a small piece of precious wood, you need to take special precautions to secure the piece and to protect your fingers.

The safest way to work with small pieces is on a sled. It allows you to hold the piece down with a stick that "bridges" over from a piece of riser scrap of the same thickness as your workpiece. That way, your fingers are out of the danger zone and the sled supports both parts of the piece throughout the cut for safety. If you don't have a sled, another option would be to set up the cut in a similar fashion against a miter gauge fence that

This small ebony workpiece can be secured for a cut by holding it down on a crosscut sled using a piece of scrap that bridges over from a piece of riser scrap.

Bridge-clamping can be done against a miter gauge fence that extends all the way to the blade.

When crosscutting live-edge slabs on a sled, shim or tack support-spacers in place to ensure that the board sits securely throughout the cut.

Long stock may require additional feed support. Here, an auxiliary stand supports the left end of the board while a support stick keeps the right-hand end from tipping off the sled.

extends all the way to the blade. For safety and accuracy, face the fence with fine sandpaper to prevent sideways slippage.

Rough Crosscutting

There will be times when you need to crosscut a board with a crook, as you might when you're rough cutting a large plank into the smaller pieces you need for a project. You could make the cuts with a portable circular saw or jigsaw, but they can also be done on the tablesaw using a crosscut sled. The critical concern is to place the convex edge against the fence. If you place the concave edge against the fence, the board will collapse at the end of the cut, pinching on the blade and startling you.

Cutting a live-edge slab can present a bit more of a challenge when it has a snaky shape instead of a distinct one-directional crook. For proper support, each half of the board should be supported near the blade and near the far end of the fence, if necessary, to prevent collapse at the end of the cut. In this case, you can shim the edge to support the slab or span the gaps with support spacers, temporarily tacking them into the board near its edge.

Large Pieces

Crosscutting large boards requires a large sliding table or crosscut sled. With a large sliding table, it's a simple matter of loading the stock on the table, lining up the cut, and pushing the table forward. A crosscut sled will do the job nicely too, although you may need to set up additional stock supports. When making cuts with a long sled, provide infeed support under the sled to keep it from tipping off the saw while loading it.

CROSSCUTTING CROOKED BOARDS

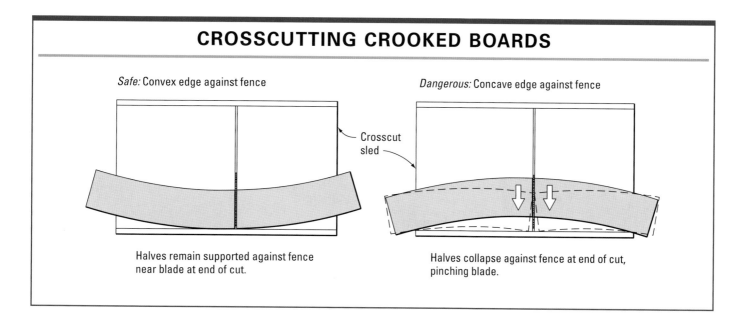

Safe: Convex edge against fence

Dangerous: Concave edge against fence

Crosscut sled

Halves remain supported against fence near blade at end of cut.

Halves collapse against fence at end of cut, pinching blade.

► See "Crosscut-Sled Support Arm" on p. 44.

Full-Size Sheet Goods

If, like most of us, you don't have a saw equipped with a large sliding table, crosscutting full-size 4-ft. by 8-ft. sheet goods can be tricky. It is possible to crosscut sheets by feeding them against the rip fence, but most large rip fences are limited to about a 50-in. capacity. This allows you to crosscut a sheet in half, though, which is a fairly common operation. You just have to set up feed support so the panel doesn't topple during the cut. For safe, accurate feeding, place your hands in the center of each panel half, and keep your feed pressure moving straight forward. Once the piece is cut in half, sawing the halves into smaller pieces is much easier.

[TIP] "Crosscutting" of sheet goods (which don't have a singular grain direction), as used here, means sawing across the narrower dimension of the stock.

When cutting wide panels on a long sled, provide infeed support under the sled to prevent it from tipping when setting up for the cut.

Crosscutting a sheet of plywood in half can be accomplished by running it along the rip fence. Provide adequate support for the piece you're cutting free.

You can crosscut full-size sheet goods that are too big for the tablesaw by guiding a portable circular saw with a shopmade straightedge guide.

PORTABLE CIRCULAR SAW GUIDE

1/2-in. by 4-in. by 50-in. plywood fence

Workpiece

Line up edge of guide with workpiece cutline.

Plywood base panel, 1/4 in. thick

To make jig, attach oversize base panel to plywood fence, then trim panel to final size by guiding saw against fence.

roughly to size with a portable circular saw or jigsaw first. It doesn't have to be a perfect cut. Just make it a bit larger than you need, and trim it to final size on the tablesaw afterward when it's a more manageable size.

I usually make the cut with my portable circular saw, guiding it with a custom-made plywood straightedge, as shown in the drawing at left. If you have a freestanding outfeed table, you can pull it away from the saw enough to create a cutting channel, with both pieces of the sheet fully supported during and after the cut.

[TIP] **To prevent tearout from a portable circular saw, score through the top layer of veneer on the cutline using a sharp knife.**

Thin Stock

Thin stock, such as plastic laminate, must be held down against the saw table or the blade will try to push it upward, leading to jumpy cuts and shattered edges. No problem. Just cover the sheet with a piece of heavier scrap, placing it right at the cutline. When using

There are times, however, when you need to crosscut just a small length from a full-size sheet. Rather than try to support the majority of the sheet as it hangs off the edge of the saw, it's usually best to cut the piece

To cut a piece of plastic laminate using the miter gauge, hold down the stock with a scrap of wood.

The cleanest and safest way to saw thin materials is with a crosscut sled, covering both sides of the material with scrap wood.

When crosscutting bevels, make sure the offcut is oriented toward the underside of the tilted blade.

a miter gauge, you'll be able to support only half of the cut, which is usually fine, especially if the workpiece isn't very wide.

However, the most secure approach is to make the cut using a crosscut sled. This way, both pieces can be covered, and there is no offcut to fall free because both pieces travel with the sled. This is definitely the best approach when cutting wider panels that would be awkward to handle with the miter gauge.

See "Crosscut Sleds and Miter Sleds" on p. 31.

Crosscutting Bevels

When crosscutting bevels, the same rules apply as when ripping them. That is, the offcut should be oriented toward the underside of the tilted blade rather than trapping the finished bevel on the underside, where it could be burned or overcut if it springs up against the blade. Beveling the ends of large panels is best done with a sliding table on a right-tilt saw. Lacking that, I use a single-runner sled, as shown on p. 160.

See "Ripping A Bevel" on p. 129.

See "Beveling on a Sled" on p. 160.

A

B

Simple Crosscut with a Miter Gauge

Crosscutting usually involves sawing a piece to final length while squaring up both ends in the process. For the cleanest cut, begin by installing a zero-clearance insert plate, which will minimize exit tearout by supporting the wood fibers right next to the cut. Raise the blade between ¼ in. and ⅜ in. above the stock.

▶ See "Making a Zero-Clearance Throat Plate" on p. 38.

C

D

Trim one end of the stock square, making sure there is some meat on both sides of the blade to prevent sideways deflection **(A)**. Measuring from the end you just cut, mark the piece to final length **(B)**. Use a square to extend the cutline across the face and down the leading edge of the stock. With the saw off, align the blade with the cutline **(C)**. With the stock backed away from the blade, turn on the saw and begin the cut, traveling slowly at the start until you're sure the blade is following the cutline perfectly **(D)**. Pick up speed, feeding the piece quickly and at a consistent rate throughout the entire cut **(E)**. Make sure to keep a firm grip on the stock and miter gauge to prevent sideways slipping.

[TIP] Don't try to knock away a small off-cut with the blade spinning. Turn the saw off first.

E

F

Once the piece has been cut through, slide the stock away from the blade just enough to prevent it from grazing the blade on the return stroke, then pull it and the miter gauge back to the starting position **(F)**.

Simple Crosscut with a Sled

Panels are best crosscut using a sled, which provides solid support for larger workpieces. Lay out your cutline, extending it down the leading edge of the panel. Extend it a little way across the face so you can gauge the initial cutting progress, making sure you're staying on the line. When aligning the cutline to the blade, I place my right hand against the end of the board near the sled kerf with my left hand pinching the board and my left index finger against the edge of the sled **(A)**. This allows easy shifting of the panel sideways as necessary to fine-tune the cut alignment.

When you're ready, turn on the saw and pull the board tightly against the fence with your other hand behind it pushing the sled forward **(B)**. At the end of the cut, pull the board slightly away from the blade to prevent grazing it on the return stroke **(C)**. Hold the board against the fence as you return the sled to its starting position **(D)**.

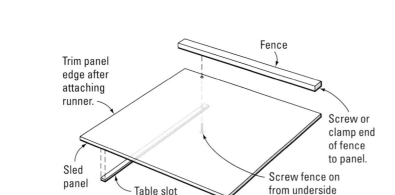

Trim panel edge after attaching runner.

Fence

Screw or clamp end of fence to panel.

Sled panel

Table slot runner

Screw fence on from underside of panel.

Beveling on a Sled

Crosscutting a bevel on a wide panel can be done easily with a single-runner sled. It's nothing more than a panel attached to a runner, with a fence that's attached with a screw at one end and a clamp at the other **(A)**. The fence pivots on the screw to allow cutting bevels on both square and angled pieces.

To bevel your workpiece, first cut it to finished size, which allows using the finished ends as a cutting reference. Mark the bevel on the leading edge of the panel. Place the panel on the sled, and align the cutline with the blade **(B)**. Hold the panel firmly down and against the fence. Feed it slowly forward until you're sure that the blade is perfectly intersecting the corner, creating a knife edge without shortening the board **(C)**. When you see that you're on track, speed up the feed rate, moving the piece at a consistent clip to the end of the cut **(D)**. This should produce a neat, crisp bevel all across the panel end **(E)**.

Multiples with a Stop Block

When sawing multiple workpieces to the same length, it's important to handle the pieces in an organized fashion and to use a stop block for efficiency and accuracy. Before crosscutting to final length, make sure all the pieces have been dressed to thickness and width. Stack the pieces to be cut, and trim one end of each piece **(A)**. As always, make sure there is wood on both sides of the saw kerf to prevent the blade from deflecting. A thinly sliced offcut will be blown away by the blade, saving you the trouble of stopping the saw to remove it.

Measuring from the trimmed end, mark one of the pieces to length **(B)**. Then carry the cutline down the leading edge of the piece. Place the stock against the miter gauge fence and align the mark with the blade. Take a quick nip-cut to make sure the stock is aligned properly, then carefully back it away from the blade. Butt a stop block against the end, and clamp it in place **(C)**. Now cut all your pieces to final size, butting each one firmly against the stop block to make the cut **(D)**.

Multiples with a Flip Stop

A flip stop provides better efficiency than using a simple stop block clamped to a fence. Using a clamped stop block requires first trimming one end of all the pieces, then setting up the stop block to cut the opposite ends. Using a flip stop offers the efficiency of handling each piece only once.

Trim one end of your first piece square, making sure to create an offcut to prevent blade deflection **(A)**. After the cut, turn the piece end for end and mark it to length, measuring from the end you just cut **(B)**. Align the cutline with the blade and butt the flip stop against the opposite end **(C)**. Holding the piece firmly against the stop and fence, cut it to final length. Every subsequent cut is fast and easy. Simply trim the first end with the stop up, and the second with it down.

Multiples with a Fence Block

If you need to cut a series of short pieces from long stock, you can use a miter gauge in concert with a set-up block clamped to your rip fence. The set-up block prevents the workpiece from getting trapped between the blade and the rip fence, which invites kickback.

Begin by cutting one end of your stock square. Then mark your cutline for the first piece. Place the piece against the miter gauge fence and align the cutline with the edge of the teeth that faces *away* from the miter gauge **(A)**. Clamp the stock to the miter gauge, and pull it forward of the blade a few inches. Clamp a thick, wide piece of squared stock to the fence, with the block's leading end approximately aligned with the leading edge of the workpiece **(B)**. Carefully slide the rip fence over until the set-up block touches the end of the stock, and lock the fence in place.

> ⚠ **WARNING To prevent kickback, it's critical that the workpiece fully passes the set-up block before completing the cut.**

Turn on the saw and push the workpiece forward, making sure it maintains firm contact against the miter gauge fence **(C, D)**. When the cut is complete, clear away the freed piece **(E)**. (If you're not comfortable doing this with the blade running, shut down the saw first.) Repeat the same maneuver until all your pieces have been cut **(F)**.

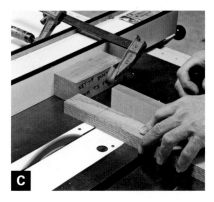

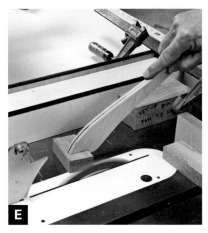

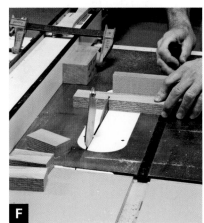

A

B

Multiples with a Sled

Identical multiples can be cut using a sled instead of a miter gauge. After squaring one end of every piece, mark a cutline to final length on the first piece. Clamp a stop block to the sled fence at the end of the stock. Make the cut holding the piece tightly against the fence and stop block **(A)**. At the end of the cut, continue to hold the stock firmly against the stop block for the return stroke **(B)**.

[TIP] Cut a small "dust-reservoir" chamfer on the bottom inside corner of the stop block to ensure solid contact with the block.

To cut longer pieces, you can outfit your sled with an extension fence that allows clamping of a stop block at some distance away from the sled **(C)**.

▶ See "Sled Extension Bar" on p. 45.

C

Jigs for Joinery

Sacrificial Fence

➤ Sacrificial Fence with Mounting Board (p. 175)

Tenons

➤ Tenoning Jig (p. 176)

Miters

➤ Tongued Spline Miter Jig (p. 177)

➤ Keyed Frame Miter Jig (p. 178)

➤ Keyed Miter Cradle (p. 179)

Finger Joints

➤ Finger Joint Jig (p. 180)

T HE TABLESAW IS A GREAT MACHINE for cutting an enormous variety of joints, as shown in Section 10. However, to get started, a few things need to be in order: Your stock needs to be prepared properly, joints have to be laid out accurately, and you'll need certain jigs and accessories for particular jobs. Of course, your saw also needs to be tuned properly and outfitted with the right blade for the job.

In this section, I discuss the general principles for preparing and laying out your workpieces to ensure clean, tight joints with little or no tearout. I also cover crucial joint-making jigs that no serious woodworker should be without. Don't worry about the jigs costing you a lot of money; I show you

how to make them yourself. I've already covered saw tune-up procedures and blade selection.

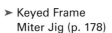
➤ For blade selection advice, see Section 3.

➤ For tune-up instructions, see Section 6.

Preparing the Stock

In general, joinery is cut after the project parts have been milled, or *dressed*, straight and square to their final thickness, width, and length. Keep in mind that in most cases you'll want to cut joints while the stock is in its squared form, before any further shaping is done such as cutting curves in legs or aprons. That's because you'll often need the straight edges for registration against your rip fence, miter gauge, or jig.

▶ See "Dressing Roughsawn Stock" on p. 209.

Milling Set-Up Pieces

When milling your workpieces, it's crucial to make some extra stock for set-up purposes. The set-up pieces usually need to be exactly the same thickness (and maybe the same width) as your final pieces. But don't expect to simply crosscut a short set-up piece from the end of a part that you've cut oversize in length. You'll want to make sure that the piece is long enough to hold safely while cutting and that it doesn't include any planer or jointer snipe that could throw off your setup. If you measure from the sniped face, your marking may be off by as much as the depth of the snipe.

[TIP] A set-up piece need not be the same species of wood as the workpiece.

Minimizing Tearout

Tearout can be a problem when cutting joints. Wood fibers that aren't supported on the bottom or backside of a cut can be torn away, leaving a ratty-looking surface. Your work can really suffer from this because it's nearly impossible to repair. Puttying or patching it is just extra work that never looks good in the end, no matter how carefully it's done. Best to just avoid the problem to begin with. Here are a few good solutions.

Make sure that set-up pieces don't include any snipe (as shown on the foreground piece), which can cause inaccuracies in your layouts.

Sacrificial Backers

A sacrificial backer supports the wood fibers adjacent to the blade, preventing them from being torn free as the teeth push through the workpiece. A backer can be employed in a number of circumstances. I always use one on my tenoning jig to prevent blowout at the end of the cut when sawing tenons or open mortises. Same thing applies when sawing slots for a keyed frame miter. The orientation of the grain and angle of tooth attack at the exit point invite serious tearout that would be painfully obvious in the finished piece, even if filled with putty.

A zero-clearance throat plate is basically a sacrificial backer. It can help reduce tearout on joinery, especially on tenon shoulders and other cross-grain cuts. When cutting joints using a crosscut sled, the sled bottom serves as a zero-clearance insert or backer. However, the slot may widen over time if you've used different blades,

Using a backer between your workpiece and a tenoning jig fence prevents tearout on the exit side of the cut.

The open mortise in the foreground was cut without a backer, resulting in tearout at the upper end of the cut. The one in the background was cut against a backer.

This jig for cutting keyed miter slots includes a replaceable backer that's screwed to the right-hand fence to eliminate exit tearout.

which somewhat compromises support of the wood fibers right next to the blade. To reestablish zero-clearance tolerances, you can cover the sled with a thin plywood or hardboard panel.

▶ See "Zero-Clearance Throat Plates" on p. 28.

▶ SAWBLADES FOR JOINERY

Joinery involves lots of crosscutting and ripping operations. Sawing the cheeks of a tenon is a rip cut, while sawing its shoulders is a crosscut. A miter is somewhere between a rip cut and a crosscut. And so on. So what kind of blade do you use for joinery? Appropriately enough, a good-quality all-purpose blade will do the trick. As discussed earlier, a 40-tooth or 50-tooth ATB blade will not only perform your regular ripping and crosscutting chores nicely but will also serve nicely for cutting joints. For the neatest, best-fitting joints, get a premium-quality blade. Don't stint on the cost of this important workhorse. And make sure to keep the blade sharp and clean.

▶ For more on sawblades, see Section 3.

A zero-clearance throat plate will minimize tearout on the underside of a workpiece when crosscutting tenon shoulders and other joints on the flat.

horizontal members to the case side, while a rabbet is usually cut into the rear edges to accommodate a back panel. The exit side of a dado (which is a crosscut) will often produce tearout. In this case, it's easily removed by making the long-grain rabbet cut afterward. Also keep in mind that tearout on the

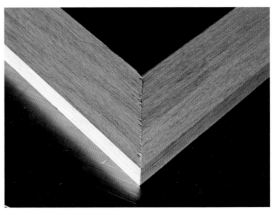

The left piece of this miter joint shows exit tearout, which wouldn't be evident if the piece had been cut good-face up, like the one at the right.

Put Your Best Face Forward

The simplest way to deal with tearout is to orient it so it will be either hidden in the finished project or shaped away later in the production process. Get used to handling your workpieces so that the blade teeth will enter the face of the stock that will be the most exposed in the finished piece. For example, when cutting drawer fronts to length, orient the drawer face upward so any tearout will be on the underside/inside of the piece. The same holds true for miters or any other end cut that will butt against another piece.

First Cuts First

Sometimes you have the opportunity to remove tearout when making a subsequent cut. A perfect example of this is when cutting joints in a cabinet side. Dadoes are commonly used to join shelves and other

Cross-grain tearout on shelf dadoes can easily be cleaned up by making the rabbet for the cabinet back later.

end of a rail will often be removed when a tenon or other joint is cut into that end of the piece.

Planning for Strong Joints

Strong joints depend on three basic factors: face-grain to face-grain glue contact, a good fit, and proper assembly. So to ensure long-lasting projects, your joints need to be designed correctly, cut properly, and glued up with care. I couldn't possibly go into all of the specifics in this book, but here's the upshot.

Face-Grain Contact

Due to the structure of wood, a glued joint depends on intimate contact between two or more face-grain (or "long-grain") surfaces. Conversely, an end-grain surface provides a very weak bond. To test this out, try gluing two sticks together end to end, letting the glue cure, and then banging the assembly over the edge of a table. The joint will snap without much effort. Butt joining an end-grain surface to a face-grain surface doesn't offer a whole lot more strength. However, if you glue together two face-grain surfaces (two sticks in an X-shape, for example), you'll have a very hard time breaking them apart.

Many joints also incorporate a mechanical connection. For example, a mortise-and-tenon joint gains its strength partly from the face-grain contact between the tenon cheeks and the mortise walls and partly from the mortise's physical capture of the tenon. Same thing with finger joints. The face-grain on the sides of the fingers mate, while the mechanical interlock prevents lateral movement.

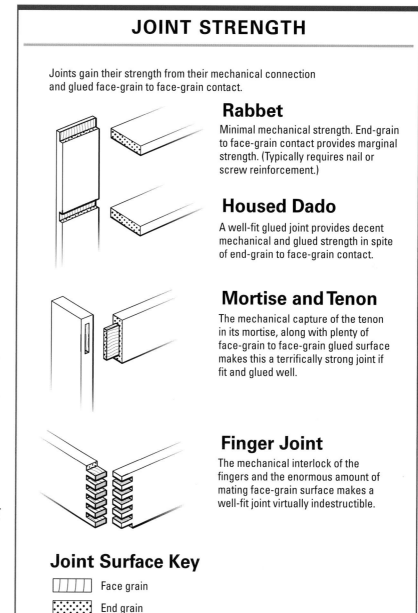

JOINT STRENGTH

Joints gain their strength from their mechanical connection and glued face-grain to face-grain contact.

Rabbet

Minimal mechanical strength. End-grain to face-grain contact provides marginal strength. (Typically requires nail or screw reinforcement.)

Housed Dado

A well-fit glued joint provides decent mechanical and glued strength in spite of end-grain to face-grain contact.

Mortise and Tenon

The mechanical capture of the tenon in its mortise, along with plenty of face-grain to face-grain glued surface makes this a terrifically strong joint if fit and glued well.

Finger Joint

The mechanical interlock of the fingers and the enormous amount of mating face-grain surface makes a well-fit joint virtually indestructible.

Joint Surface Key

▯▯▯▯ Face grain

▦▦▦ End grain

Joints such as a simple housed dado or a dado and rabbet don't offer any face-grain contact and depend on a combination of glue and mechanical connection for strength. These joints are adequate for many applications, but must fit together very well for longevity.

REINFORCING JOINTS WITH SPLINES

A butted miter joint is weak because of its mating end-grain surfaces. Splines offer a great solution for reinforcement.

Splined Frame Miter

The spline's face grain mates with the face grain of its slot to create great glued strength. *Note:* Make sure the grain in the spline runs perpendicular to the miter cuts.

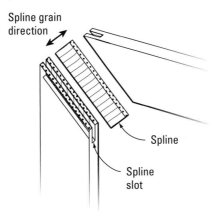

Spline grain direction

Spline

Spline slot

Splined Case Miter

Inserting a spline into a case miter groove provides good mechanical and gluing strength to an otherwise weak joint.

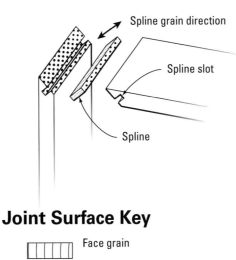

Spline grain direction

Spline slot

Spline

Joint Surface Key

▦	Face grain
▨	End grain

[TIP] Keep in mind that the edge of a piece of plywood may be nearly half face grain, offering greater gluing strength than the end of a solid-wood board.

A miter is a slice made diagonally across the grain, but the joint surface has gluing qualities more like end grain than face grain. For durability, a miter joint must be reinforced. One of the best approaches is to install a spline or splines to create face-grain glue surfaces as well as a mechanical interlock.

A Good Fit

For both mechanical strength and glue strength, a joint needs to fit like a glove. You should be able to push it together with some resistance, but not enough to require a lot of coaxing with a mallet or clamp. On the other hand, if the two parts clack together, the joint is too loose. And don't count on the glue to act as a filler; it's not meant to. A loose joint is a compromised joint.

When cutting joints on the tablesaw, use a set-up piece to get the fit right before chewing into your good stock. When setting up for the cut, begin with a well laid out joint. It's a wise practice to begin by sawing just a bit shy of your layout lines, then making test cuts, gradually sneaking up on the cut until it's perfect. (If you overcut to begin with, you'll have to start over with a fresh set-up piece.) Once you have the fit you're after, register the setup by locking in your fence, stop blocks, and other adjustments. Then make the appropriate cuts in your workpieces.

Jigging Up

There's no question about it: Joinery means jigs. There are a few operations, such as cutting dadoes and grooves, that can be performed using only the tablesaw rip fence, but many require using a miter gauge, sled, or other jig. Fortunately, it's not difficult to build most of the jigs you'll need to produce perfect joints. Some are dead simple to make and use, whereas others may take an afternoon to construct. No matter. The time invested in building a good jig pays off in spades. Jigs are fun to make, and there's an endless variety, as seen in woodworking books and magazines. I'll discuss here a few that are crucial to expanding your joint-making repertoire.

Sacrificial Fence

When cutting rabbets with a dado head, it's often necessary to bury a small portion of the blade in a sacrificial fence to allow you to cut right to the end of the workpiece without scarring your rip fence. It's important that a sacrificial fence be straight, flat, and of consistent thickness because feeding a workpiece along a curvy or tapered fence can spoil a cut.

Attaching a sacrificial fence can be a simple matter of clamping or screwing it to your rip fence. However, clamps can impede push sticks, and you may not like the idea of screwing into your expensive rip fence. In that case, you can screw the sacrificial fence to a mounting board that clamps to your rip

To avoid overcutting a joint, begin by taking a "nip cut" a bit shy of your layout line. Then adjust the workpiece position and blade height as necessary to make a perfect cut.

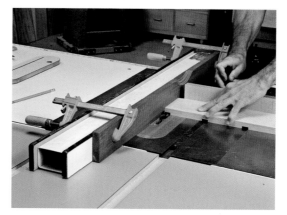

When using a dado head to cut all the way to the end of a workpiece, use a sacrificial fence to avoid scarring your saw's rip fence.

By adding a mounting board to your sacrificial fence, you can keep your clamps out of the way of your push stick.

A typical commercial tenoning jig can easily be adjusted to hold work at any angle from 90 degrees to about 40 degrees.

fence. When the sacrificial fence needs to be replaced or switched out, you can just screw a new one to the mounting board.

▶ See "Sacrificial Fence with Mounting Board" on p. 175.

Jigs For Tenoning

The tablesaw is a superb machine for cutting tenons, open mortises, and other joints that require sawing into the end of a piece of stock. But you need a jig to hold the workpiece on end as you push it past the blade. Commercially available tenoning jigs will do the job nicely and allow you to hold a workpiece at a variety of angles, which can be very useful if you do a lot of angled joinery. However, if you don't want to spend the $100 or so for one, you can easily make your own carriage jig if you have a Biesemeyer-style fence.

▶ See "Tenoning Jig" on p. 176.

There's no shortage of good designs for shopmade tenoning jigs in woodworking books and magazines. Many ride the rip fence, but some are designed to ride in a miter gauge slot in case your rip fence won't easily accommodate a carriage-style jig.

Miter Sled

Despite their simplicity, miters can be some of the fussiest joints to cut well. If you're just a degree or so off, the joint won't close up well. And since you're usually joining a frame of some sort, the error is likely to show up on all four corners. It's not just the 45-degree angle that has to be correct; if the face of the joint isn't square to the face

A carriage-style tenoning jig is easy to make and will allow you to cut tenon cheeks, open-end mortises, spline slots, and lots of other cuts that require standing a workpiece on end.

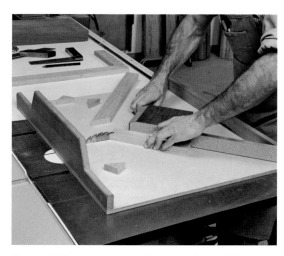

A carefully constructed miter sled with two fences set at 90 degrees to each other and at 45 degrees to the blade ensures perfect miters every time.

Because the fence on this commercial tenoning jig angles only backward, spline slots must be perfectly centered for efficient cutting.

of the stock, the resulting frame may twist during assembly.

You can use a miter gauge to saw miters, but the cuts are much easier to make using a sled. The best kind of miter sled incorporates two fences set at exactly 90 degrees to each other and at 45 degrees to the blade. If you make a lot of frame miters, I strongly recommend a miter sled.

▶ See "Frame Miter Sled" on p. 48.

Spline Jigs

Spline joinery is an essential way to connect wood and offers a great way to reinforce miter joints. The tablesaw is an excellent tool for cutting spline slots in miters but requires the use of a jig. A commercial tenoning jig can be used to saw slots for a tongued miter, but the slot must be perfectly centered for efficient work. That's because half the slots will be cut with the workpiece "show" face against the jig and half with it away. I gen-

erally prefer to use a shopmade, twin-fence carriage jig, which creates perfect alignment with even offset slots.

▶ See "Splined Frame Miter" on p. 193.

This spline-slotting jig includes a twin fence on the opposite side for quickly slotting the mating miters, even when making offset slots.

A jig for cutting slots for keyed miters carries the glued-up frame across the blade at 45 degrees.

A finger joint jig is quite easy to make and allows you to cut strong, attractive box and drawer joints.

Slotting for keyed miter joints requires using a jig that carries the assembled frame or case across the blade. Both jigs are easy to make and well worth the effort.

▶ See "Keyed Frame Miter Jig" on p. 178

Jig for Finger Joints

Another very useful joint that you'll need to jig up for is a finger joint. Its interlocking fingers provide a lot of long-grain glue surface as well as a strong mechanical connection, creating a nearly unbreakable joint. It is often used to build drawers and decorative boxes. The joint is easy to cut using a simple shopmade jig.

A cradle jig is necessary to hold boxes and other casework at the proper angle when cutting slots for keyed miter joints.

▶ See "Finger Joint Jig" on p. 180.

Sacrificial Fence with Mounting Board

Joint and plane a heavy straight-grained board, leaving it at least 1¾ in. thick. Cut it to match the height and approximate length of your rip fence. Clamp it to your rip fence with F-clamps, leaning the bar of the clamp down against the top of the fence to create as low a profile as possible **(A)**. (Tall-standing clamps can be knuckle-bangers when feeding stock.)

Mark a line down the face of the board at the nose of each clamp **(B)**, then mark an angle that runs parallel to the jaw **(C)**. Extend the lines across the top of the board, and complete the notch layout, leaving at least ½ in. of meat against the fence **(D)**.

Cut the notches out. You can rout them or saw and chisel them. They don't have to be pretty. Drill and countersink screw holes through the rear of the board, avoiding the area near the blade. Mill a ¾-in.-thick fence the same width and length as the mounting board **(E)**. Screw the pieces together, clamp the assembly to your rip fence, and you're ready to go **(F)**.

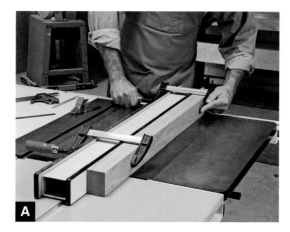

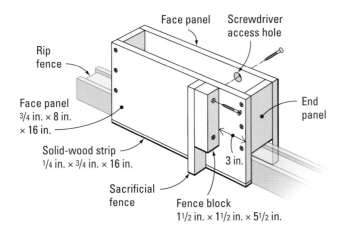

Face panel

Screwdriver access hole

Rip fence

Face panel
3/4 in. × 8 in. × 16 in.

End panel

Solid-wood strip
1/4 in. × 3/4 in. × 16 in.

3 in.

Sacrificial fence

Fence block
1 1/2 in. × 1 1/2 in. × 5 1/2 in.

A

B

C

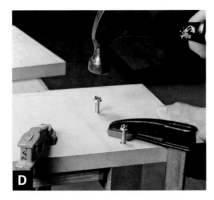

D

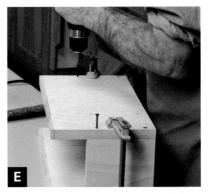

E

F

G

Tenoning Jig

Cut the two face panels from 3/4-in.-thick MDF or hardwood plywood. Clamp them to your fence and mark a piece of 3/4-in.-thick plywood to fit in between to make the end panels **(A)**. Cut the end panels to size and clamp them between the face panels on the fence to make sure the unit slides easily but without side-to-side play **(B)**. (If too tight, shim between the joints with masking tape.) Glue a 1/4-in.-thick strip of solid wood to one long edge of each face panel. This allows jointing the unit square later if necessary without harming your jointer knives.

Make the fence block, ensuring that its faces are perfectly square to each other. Lay out the clearance holes for the screws in the panel for attaching the fence block. Make sure the lower hole will clear a fully raised blade. Also lay out two screwdriver access holes in the opposite panel **(C)**. Then drill the holes, making the upper one about 1/32-in. larger in diameter to allow for slight fence angle adjustment later. Lay out and drill the clearance holes for attaching a sacrificial fence to the fence block with 2-in.-long drywall screws.

Clamp the fence block in place, square to the bottom edge of the panel. Slip the screws in their holes, and tap them lightly to mark the center hole in the fence block **(D)**. Then drill the pilot holes in it using the drill press.

Drill pilot holes and screw the face panels to the end panels **(E)**. With the unit on your rip fence, make sure the face panel is square to the table. If necessary, run the unit across your jointer to square up the bottom edges. Screw the fence block in place **(F)**, then attach a 3/4-in.-thick sacrificial fence **(G)**, making sure its bearing face is square to the table.

Tongued Spline Miter Jig

The body of this carriage jig is constructed in the same fashion as the body of the tenoning jig shown on the previous page. To work properly, it's important that the carriage faces are the same thickness and very flat. If necessary to flatten the faces, you can screw them to an interior panel that's cut to the exact width of the end panels **(A)**. Make sure the faces of the assembled carriage are square to the saw table. If necessary, run the unit across your jointer, pressing the panel firmly against the jointer fence **(B)**.

Cut two fences, each about 10 in. long, mitering each end. On the drill press, bore clearance holes through each for the screws that will hold the sacrificial fences. At the same time, bore the holes for attaching each fence to its side of the jig. Countersink the holes enough to allow a 2-in. screw to get good bite into its panel or sacrificial fence.

Screw one fence to each face panel, using a miter square to ensure that it sits at 45 degrees **(C)**. The fences should be mounted parallel to each other on opposite faces of the jig. Make a sacrificial fence, bevel one end, and screw it to the "right-hand" fence as shown **(D)**.

▶ **For how to use the jig, see p. 193.**

A

B

C

D

A

B

C

D

Keyed Frame Miter Jig

This carriage jig is very similar to the tongued spline miter jig on p. 177, except that both angled fences are on the same side of the jig. For convenience, I mounted these fences on the opposite side of my tenoning jig. The two fences sit at 90 degrees to each other and at 45 degrees to the panel. The key here is to lay out the fences (with the sacrificial fence attached) so that they will carry the corner of an assembled frame just above the saw table for slotting.

▶ See "Tenoning Jig" on p. 176.

Dress a piece of 1½-in.-sq. stock about 20 in. long for the fences, and make a piece ¾-in. by 1½-in. by 12-in. for the sacrificial fence. Cut the right-hand fence to about 9 in. long, miter each end, and drill the clearance holes for attaching the sacrificial fence. Place the fence in position on its panel, with the bottom end about ¾ in. up from the bottom panel edge **(A)**. When it's aligned, clamp it in place. Next, put the sacrificial fence against the right-hand fence, and place a square against it with the apex of the square about ⅛ in. from the bottom of the panel. Clamp the square in place and locate the left-hand fence against it, with its end about ¾ in. from the panel bottom **(B)**. Mark the left-hand fence **(C)**, then cut it to length.

With the fences both clamped to the panel, lay out and drill the holes for attaching them to the panel. Then screw everything in place **(D)**.

Keyed Miter Cradle

Base the sled width on your saw, extending it at least 1 in. past each miter gauge slot. Cut the pieces for the sled panel and cradle sides from ½-in.-thick hardwood plywood. Rip some solid wood for the cradle supports, cutting the stock long enough for safe handling, then miter and crosscut the pieces to length. Saw the runners from straight-grained hardwood, milling them slightly thinner than the slot depth but wide enough to fit snugly from side to side. Cut the blade guard to size and miter one end at 45 degrees.

Place the runners in the miter gauge slots, shimming them flush to the tabletop. Center the sled over them, and register the rip fence against one edge. Mark the center of the runners on the panel, and drive in a few brads, leaving the heads proud for removal later **(A)**. Flip the sled over, and attach the runners with countersunk screws driven through the runners **(B)**. Now check the fit of the sled in the slots, scraping or sanding any spots that bind in the slots.

Next, bevel one edge of each cradle side to 45 degrees and attach the sides to the supports. To do this, clamp a thick, straight board across your bench for support, and place what will be the leading edge of the sled against it. Mark the support centerlines across the panel, then place the rear supports on the lines. Tack or screw a cradle side to the supports while butting them up against the support board **(C)**. Turn the panel around and do the same for the opposite supports **(D)**. Position the unit upside down against the board, and tack or screw through the panel into the supports **(E)**. Glue the blade guard in place. Finito!

▶ For how to use the jig, see p. 195.

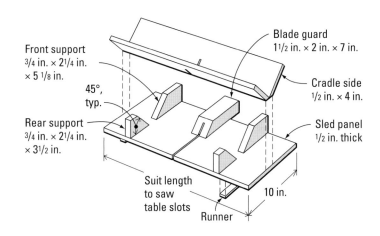

Front support
¾ in. × 2¼ in. × 5⅛ in.

45°, typ.

Rear support
¾ in. × 2¼ in. × 3½ in.

Blade guard
1½ in. × 2 in. × 7 in.

Cradle side
½ in. × 4 in.

Sled panel
½ in. thick

Suit length to saw table slots

Runner

10 in.

A

B

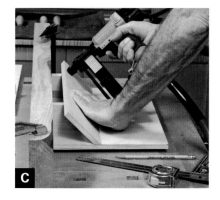

C

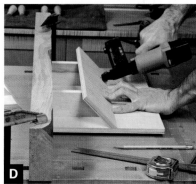

D

E

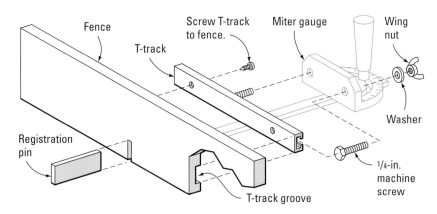

Fence

T-track

Screw T-track
to fence.

Miter gauge

Wing
nut

Registration
pin

T-track groove

Washer

¼-in.
machine
screw

Finger Joint Jig

In its most basic form, a finger joint jig is simply a fence with a registration pin projecting from its bottom edge. To guide the fence past the blade, you attach it to either a miter gauge or a sled. The crucial feature is that the fence be adjustable side to side, which allows you to make perfectly fitting joints.

I made my 1-in. by 5-in. by 20-in. fence from solid hardwood, but you could use ¾-in. hardwood plywood instead. Just make sure it's straight and flat. The registration pin needs to be exactly as thick as your intended fingers. It should be no wider (taller) than the thickness of the stock you intend to join. In this example, I'm making a jig for cutting ¼-in.-wide fingers in stock no less than ½ in. thick, so my pin is ¼ in. by $^{17}/_{32}$ in. by 2 in.

To make the fence adjustable from side to side, mount a short section of ¾-in.-wide aluminum T-track into a groove in the rear of the fence. The T-track accepts the hex heads of a pair of ¼-in. cap screws that project through holes in the miter gauge head. Wing nuts on the screws hold the track and fence to the miter gauge. The track doesn't need to be much longer than the width of your miter gauge head.

A

After cutting the fence to size, saw a groove to accept the T-track. For accurate groove layout, I temporarily mount the track on the miter gauge, stand the fence against it, and trace the groove edge **(A)**. Set up your dado head, and cut the groove for the track **(B)**.

Next, set up the dado head to match the thickness of your desired fingers/slots. I usually use a standard combination of blades—the two outer blades for ¼-in. fingers, the two outers plus a chipper for ⅜-in. fingers, and so on. This makes it easy to create the same set up in the future. Slot a piece of scrap, then make a registration pin to fit the slot exactly.

B

For safe handling when making the hardwood pin, begin with stock at least 16 in. long, and about 1¼ in. wide. I run the stock through my planer first, which gets it pretty close **(C)**, then I sand or handplane it until it fits the test slot exactly. Rip the stock to a width (height) about ⅟₃₂ in. less than the thickness of the workpieces you'll be joining **(D)**. You only need about 6 in. of length. Crosscut a 2-in.-long piece from that to serve as the pin, and keep the remaining 4 in. to use as a spacer when cutting the joints. Set the pin and spacer aside for now. [

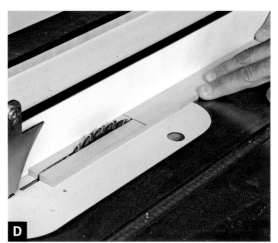

> See "Making Finger Joints" on p. 197.

[TIP] Instead of mounting the jig on a miter gauge, you can clamp it to the fence of a tablesaw crosscut sled.

Screw or epoxy the T-track into the fence so that, when mounted on the miter gauge, the center of the fence will sit 1 in. or so to the left of the cutter **(E)**. Mount the fence on the miter gauge, and cut the slot for the pin into the approximate center of the fence **(F)**. All that's left is to glue the 2-in.-long pin into its slot, and use a chisel to lightly chamfer its top edges **(G)**

Making Joints

Rabbets, Dadoes, & Grooves

Miters

Finger Joints

Mortises and Tenons

WHEN IT COMES TO CUTTING joints, the tablesaw is rivaled only by the router. There are few other tools that are capable of making such a wide variety of joints, including rabbets, grooves, dadoes, tenons, miters, and lap joints. There is not enough space here to cover all the variations, but I show you the basics. From there, you'll be able to branch out and tackle more advanced work on your own.

Please be sure to read Section 9 too, which includes tips and advice on preparing stock for joinery and using backers to minimize tearout. The Section 9 projects also show you how to build jigs for making some of the joints introduced in this section.

Rabbets, Dadoes, & Grooves

Rabbets are used in a number of situations. You'll often see an *end rabbet* where a drawer side meets the drawer front or the side of

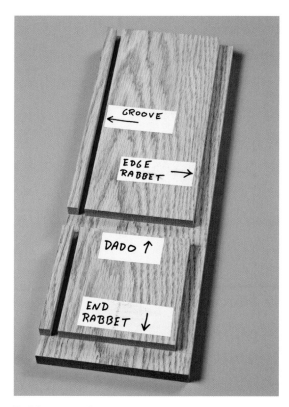

In a tongue-and-groove joint (bottom), the groove mates with a tongue cut into the adjacent piece. With a splined edge joint (top), a spline spans two mating grooves.

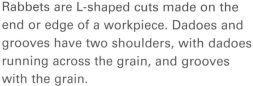

Rabbets are L-shaped cuts made on the end or edge of a workpiece. Dadoes and grooves have two shoulders, with dadoes running across the grain, and grooves with the grain.

a case mates with the top and bottom. Due to the lack of face-grain gluing surface in solid wood, this joint requires mechanical fasteners along with the glue for strength. *Edge rabbets* are often cut in the rear edges of case sides to accept the case back. Here, there is usually plenty of good face-grain to face-grain contact, so glue alone is sufficient to hold things together. You'll also see edge rabbets frequently on the rear face of door frames, cut there to accept glass or wood panels.

Dadoes are commonly used to house shelves, case partitions, and other project dividers. A well-fit joint offers mechani-

cal strength in three directions. However, because of the lack of face-grain contact between the mating members, a durable joint may require screws or other fasteners in addition to glue.

Grooves offer solid capture of drawer bottoms, case backs, and other panels. These joints are often left unglued (especially if the panel is solid wood) to allow the panel to expand and contract freely with changes in moisture content. If glue is desired, though, the joint's face grain offers a good gluing surface. Grooves are an essential element in other joinery too, such as tongue-and-groove joints and edge-spline joints.

Lap Joints

Common lap joints include the *shiplap, end lap*, and *crosslap*. Shiplap and end-lap joints are simply mating rabbet joints, while a crosslap joint consists of two mating dadoes. All of the joints provide good gluing strength because of their large face-grain contact. End laps and crosslaps are primarily used to join frame members, while shiplaps are employed to create larger panels from narrower pieces of wood.

A shiplap (bottom) and a crosslap (top front) consist of mating rabbets. The crosslap at the rear is the result of two mating dadoes.

Simple miter joints are not very strong without reinforcement by splines or mechanical fasteners.

IS A DADO HEAD REALLY NECESSARY?

While it's possible to cut dadoes, rabbets, and grooves by making multiple passes over a standard blade, it's a tedious approach, especially when cutting multiple pieces. Plus the resulting cut won't be as flat and clean as one made with a good dado head. Sometimes frugality costs too much time. If you want to make nice joints quickly, buy a good dado head.

The ridged-bottom dado at left was cut with multiple passes over a single sawblade. The flat-bottom dado was made with a single pass over a good-quality dado head.

Miters

Miters are used to connect the corners of frames and cases. While most commonly used for 90-degree corners, miters of any angle are possible by varying the measurements involved. The joint provides an attractive way to connect a molding at an angle without interrupting its profile. Compound miter cuts, which angle in two directions, can be used to create tapered cases or to join trim (such as crown molding) that sits obliquely to its reference surfaces. The problem with miters is they are inherently weak because their mating surfaces are essentially end grain. A strong, durable miter joint requires reinforcement with splines or mechanical fasteners.

Splined Miters

When a mitered door frame may take serious abuse or when it must carry the weight of a heavy glass panel, its joints need to be substantial. In those cases, it's best to

These miter joints are reinforced by splines that run completely across the joint, fitted into mating grooves. Note that the grain of the splines runs perpendicular to the glue lines.

insert a spline that runs the full length of the joint. The face grain of the spline glued to the face grain of its groove creates a very strong connection. A case miter can also be reinforced with a spline, creating a strong glued connection with mechanical strength.

Keyed Miters

Miters on picture frames and boxes can be reinforced with small splines called "keys," which intersect the corner. They provide face-grain glue contact and can serve as decorative elements when cut from a contrasting wood. The key slots are cut after the frame or box is assembled. For best results, cut the keys oversize, then trim them flush after the glue dries to create an attractive, durable joint.

Mortise-and-Tenon Joints

The mortise-and-tenon joint is ubiquitous in furniture making. Because of its strong mechanical connection and broad face-grain

Keys are small reinforcing splines that can serve as decorative elements in picture frames and boxes. Again, the spline grain runs perpendicular to the glue line.

Mortise-and-tenon joints take many forms, including the bridle joint (front), four-shoulder tenon (left), and haunched tenon (right).

The interlocking fingers on a finger joint provide a strong mechanical connection as well as plenty of face-grain glue contact.

contact surfaces, it's one of the strongest ways to connect pieces at right angles. In addition to being a superb frame joint, it's also used to connect table aprons and rails to legs and other vertical members.

The joint takes many forms. One of the most common and useful is the bridle joint, which consists of a two-shouldered tenon that inserts into an "open" mortise. What's really nice about this joint is that both the mortise and the tenon can be cut on the tablesaw. It's a very strong frame joint and easy to make. That aside, the typical mortise-and-tenon joint consists of a four-shouldered tenon that fits into an enclosed mortise. The tenon part of this joint (including *haunched* tenons and other versions) is easily and accurately cut on the tablesaw. The mortise, however, must be routed or chopped out with a chisel.

Finger Joints

A finger joint (also called a box joint) is terrifically strong because of the large amount of face-grain glue surface shared by the interlocking fingers. It's an impressive-looking connection, too, belying the fact that it's very easy to make with a simple jig. It's most often used to join decorative boxes and drawers.

Rabbets

Rabbets are easily cut in a number of ways, using either a standard blade or a dado head. An end rabbet can be cut with a standard blade in two steps. First, saw the shoulder, guiding the workpiece with the miter gauge while registering the cut using the rip fence **(A)**. Follow up by making the cheek cut while holding the stock vertically with a tenoning jig **(B)**.

The same rabbet can be made in a single stroke by using a dado head, guiding the stock on the flat with a miter gauge **(C)**. Make sure to bury the dado head in a sacrificial fence to prevent damage to your rip fence. Alternatively, you could feed the stock with a crosscut sled, registering the piece against a stop block **(D)**.

When cutting an end rabbet on a wide panel, you don't need a miter gauge to steady the stock. However, you'll still need the sacrificial fence **(E)**. To set the rabbet width (as when sawing a rabbet in a case side to accept a back panel, as shown here), use a piece of scrap the same thickness as the back panel. Adjust the rip fence so that the outermost teeth line up with the outer panel face **(F)**. Then make the cut as before, guiding the edge of the case against the sacrificial fence **(G)**.

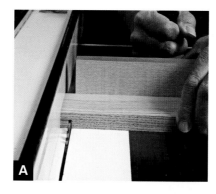

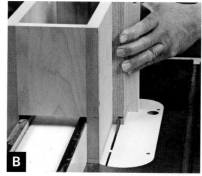

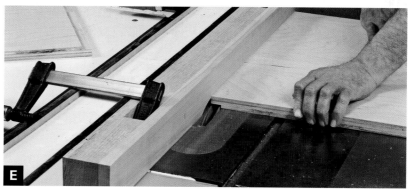

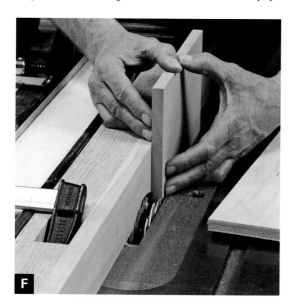

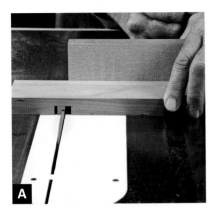

A

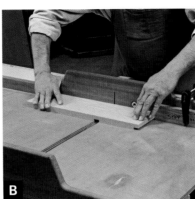

B

C

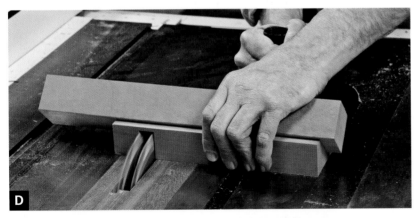

D

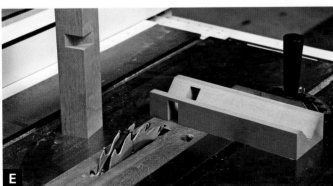

E

F

Dadoes and Grooves

Dadoes across narrow pieces can be sawn while guiding the piece with either a miter gauge or a sled. If you don't have a dado head, you can cut the joint by making a series of passes over a standard sawblade **(A)**. However, it's a tedious approach and doesn't produce a very clean cut.

When cutting dadoes in long, narrow pieces, a crosscut sled provides more stability than does a miter gauge **(B)**. Just make sure to press the stock down firmly when making the cut to ensure joints of consistent depth.

If the end of a panel is wide enough to offer stability, you can forgo a miter gauge or sled, but make sure to keep the panel firmly against the rip fence throughout the cut **(C)**. If the panel is warped at all, press it down flat against the table to ensure consistent joint depth.

Some projects, such as blanket chests, require cutting a notch into the legs to accept the corners of a bottom panel. It's no big deal to make the cut. Simply rip a V-groove into a piece of scrap to carry the workpiece across the blade, guiding it with the miter gauge **(D)**. Screwing the block to your miter gauge makes for a safer operation **(E)**.

A groove, which runs parallel to the grain instead of across it, is just as easy to cut as a dado **(F)**. It's a simple matter of adjusting the rip fence as desired, setting the blade height and keeping the stock down and against the fence as you feed it.

Tongue-and-Groove Joints

Tongue-and-groove joints can be made with a dado head or with a single blade. It's more efficient to use a dado head, so let's look at that first. Start by cutting the groove. For ¾-in.-thick stock, set up your dado head to make a ¼-in.-wide cut, and position the rip fence so the cut will be centered on the edge of your material. Mount a featherboard to apply pressure against the standing stock. Mark the "show" face of each board, then feed each piece with that face against the fence. Hold the pieces firmly down against the table as you feed them through the cut **(A)**.

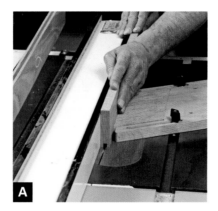

Leaving the blade at the same height, attach a sacrificial fence to your rip fence. Use the grooved edge of one of the pieces as a gauge to set up the first of two opposing rabbets that will create the tongue **(B)**. After mounting a featherboard, saw the first rabbet on all of your pieces, again applying constant downward pressure against the table **(C)**. Readjust the fence to saw the opposing rabbet, then cut all your boards, still making sure to keep the show face against the fence, which ensures a consistent joint fit regardless of any slight differences in stock thickness **(D)**.

To make the joint with a single blade, begin by sawing the groove, taking multiple passes **(E)**. Make all the first single passes before resetting the fence and featherboard for the second pass, again feeding the show face against the fence.

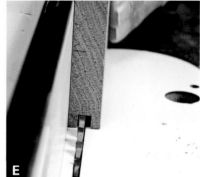

Reset the fence and featherboard to saw the first cheek cut on all the pieces (testing the fit with scrap first), then perform the same procedure to make the second cheek cut **(F)**. All that's left is to saw the shoulders. Feed with the tongue against the fence to ensure accuracy in spite of any inconsistencies in the width of your boards **(G)**.

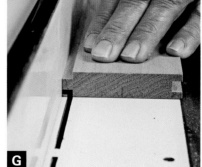

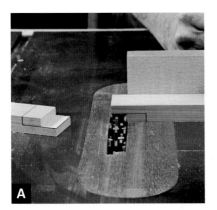
A

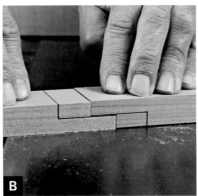
B

C

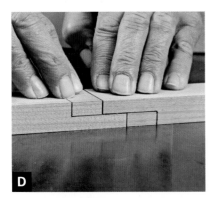
D

E

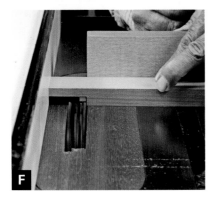
F

G

End Lap with a Dado Head

An end-lap joint is basically just a couple of wide mating rabbets of equal depth. One approach is to cut each rabbet in two steps, as shown earlier. However, I find it much quicker to use a dado head.

► **For cutting rabbets, see photos A and B on p. 187.**

Mark out the joint, then set the height of your dado head a bit shy of the line. The idea here is to creep up to a perfect fit using test pieces the same thickness as your prepared stock. Nip just a bit from the end of each piece, guiding the workpiece with the miter gauge **(A)**. Test the fit, pressing both pieces down firmly against the table **(B)**. Note the approximate amount of error, raise the blade about half that amount, and take another test cut in each piece **(C)**. Repeat if necessary until the stock faces are flush with each other **(D)**.

To set up for the shoulder cut, place the stock against the fence, aligning its outer edge with the outermost saw teeth **(E)**. (If the two pieces are of different widths, this will involve setting the fence twice to make the shoulder cuts.) Butt the end of each piece against the fence, and guide the piece past the blade with your miter gauge to make the shoulder cut **(F)**. Press the two test pieces together to make sure everything flushes up **(G)**.

Now you're ready to cut your actual workpieces. A couple quick passes with each one will do the trick.

Miters with the Miter Gauge

Begin with stock that's slightly oversize in length, with one end carefully squared up. Make two test pieces in the same dimensions as your keepers. Measuring from the squared end, draw a miter at the opposite end that marks the piece to final length. Set your miter gauge angle, line up the cutline with the blade, then clamp a stop block to your miter gauge fence, butting it against the squared end of the stock.

Saw a miter on one end of each test piece **(A)**. Hold the test pieces together to make sure they form the angle you're after **(B)**. Once you are happy with the setup, cut one end of each piece, then flip the piece end for end and saw the opposite miter **(C)**. Repeat for all pieces the same length.

Note that the miter gauge is angled away from the blade, cutting the tip of the miter first. I prefer this position because the force of the blade drives the workpiece against the stop block, preventing slippage. Also, my hand feels safer. Cutting with the miter gauge angled toward the blade gives a slightly cleaner cut since the blade is sawing with the grain **(D)**. However, the cutting force tends to pull the workpiece toward the blade, risking cutting error.

When cutting compound angles, with both the blade and the miter gauge tilted, sometimes you'll be forced by the geometry of the cut to angle the miter gauge in a particular direction **(E)**.

[VARIATION] Instead of using a miter gauge to cut odd angles, you can tack a temporary fence onto a crosscut sled at any desired angle.

A

B

C

D

E

VARIATION

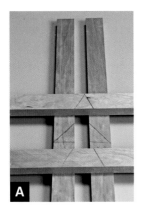

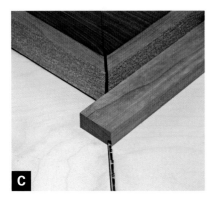

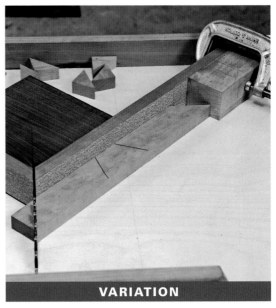

Frame Miters with Miter Sled

I find that the quickest, most accurate way to saw 45-degree frame miters is with this sled. To ensure accuracy, mating workpieces are held against the paired sled fences in their assembled orientation. So begin by marking your frame pieces with a triangle to denote their positions **(A)**.

With the pieces arranged off to the side of the sled, place the first pair on the sled with the first piece to be cut against its fence **(B)**. Take a small nip cut to be sure that the blade is precisely intersecting the apex of the joint **(C)**. Then make the cut, holding the piece firmly against the fence to prevent slippage **(D)**. Cut the mating miter in the same fashion **(E)**. Cut the rest of the joints the same way, keeping the pieces organized as you work **(F)**.

[VARIATION] If you have a number of identically sized frames to miter, set up for a perfect cut, then clamp a stop block to the fence for sawing similar pieces.

VARIATION

Splined Frame Miter

To slot miters to accept a full-length spline, I use a shopmade spline miter jig. Make sure it's outfitted with a good backer, and have on hand a hold-down board that's about ¾ in. by 4 in. by 7 in. **(A)**. The hold-down board keeps the workpiece from slipping down off the fence and serves as a backer when slotting a right-hand miter. Also make sure that your workpieces are all marked on the "show" face.

► See "Tongued Spline Miter Jig" on p. 177.

Start with the left-hand miter. Place the workpiece, show face out, against the fence with its lower end firmly on the saw table. Then position the hold-down firmly against it, and clamp the hold-down to the jig **(B)**. Locate the rip fence for the desired cut location and lock it in place. Feed past the blade, maintaining firm downward pressure as you go **(C)**. Cut all your left-hand miters with this setup, leaving the hold-down clamped in place throughout.

[TIP] After passing the blade, remove the workpiece before retracting the jig. This prevents possible overcutting of the slot on the return stroke.

Turn the jig around on the fence and set up to cut the right-hand miters. Make sure that the hold-down covers the top end of the slot location to prevent blowing out the grain there **(D)**. Feed the work in the same manner as before, holding the workpiece down on the table and against the jig face **(E)**. After cutting the slots, carefully cut stock for the splines to fit snugly in place. *Note*: the length of the spline pieces is critical—it should be exactly twice the depth of the slots. A little shy is okay, but if it's too long, the joints won't close.

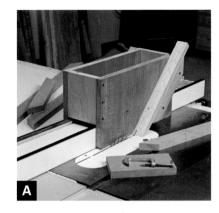
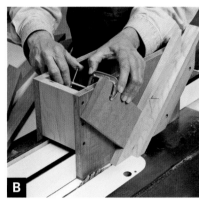

Splined Case Miter

Start by cutting the miters on the ends of the case pieces. Lay out the spline slot on the leading edge of one of the workpieces. For joint strength, locate the slot near the short end of the miter, not out near the tip. Tilt your sawblade to 45 degrees **(A)**, and use your marked workpiece to set the rip fence to locate the slot.

▶ See "Crosscutting Bevels" on p. 157.

To feed relatively narrow pieces like these, you'll need to use your miter gauge. Include a back-up stick to prevent exit tearout. Feed the piece consistently and relatively slowly across the blade, maintaining constant contact with the rip fence and table **(B)**. Repeat for each miter.

[TIP] For joint strength, the grain of the spline must run perpendicular to the miter faces.

Cut the splines from a piece of stock that's been dressed flat and squared on both ends. Use a tenoning jig to slice the splines from the outer faces of the stock **(C)**. By simply rotating the board and flipping it end for end, you can quickly cut all four splines to thickness. Saw them to the proper length using a miter gauge, with a set-up block clamped to the rip fence to help you control the splines' length **(D)**. This prevents the freed splines from kicking back when trapped between the blade and the fence. (The kickback probably won't hurt you, but it is likely to screw up your spline.)

Properly sized splines should fit their slots snugly, but without a fight. They should also completely span the mating slots while allowing the joint to close completely **(E)**.

Keyed Case Miter

A successful keyed case miter depends on accurately cut miter joints because the case must initially be assembled with unreinforced joints before cutting the key slots. Begin by making a test miter and checking it with an accurate miter square **(A)**. (Alternatively, you can place two test cuts together at 90 degrees and gauge them with a try square.)

When you're satisfied that your setup is correct, miter one end of each piece **(B)**, then the other. Use a stop block for accuracy **(C)**. Glue up the assembly, making sure it's square and that the joints are all tight **(D)**.

To saw the key slots, you'll need a way to support the assembly on its corners as you pass it over the blade. I use this joint often enough that I made a cradle specifically suited to the purpose. Alternatively, you could use a simple V-block jig, as shown in photos D & E on p. 188. Outfit the cradle jig with a backer panel to prevent tearout, then set up a stop block to register the key slots. Here, I've cut the two outer slots on each corner, and I'm setting up the stop to make the inner slots **(E)**. Holding the piece firmly against the cradle and stop, saw the slots in each corner **(F)**.

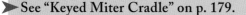
See "Keyed Miter Cradle" on p. 179.

Keyed frame miter joints can be made in essentially the same fashion but by using a different jig to cut the slots.

See the top left photo on p. 174.

A

B

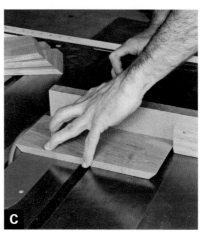
C

D

E

F

A

B

C

Making Keys

When making the splines for keyed joints, rip and plane suitably wide material to fit snugly in the slots. One approach is to simply crosscut a spline to length, and glue it into its slot in squared form, as seen in the frame at the bottom of the bottom left photo on p. 185. However, this leaves a lot of material to remove to make the key flush.

I like to make the process easier by initially sawing my keys to a slightly oversize triangular shape. That way, after gluing them in, I have only a bit of paring and planing to flush them up. Here's the approach: After preparing a long strip of spline material, set your miter gauge to 45 degrees, and clamp a wide set-up block to your rip fence. Saw a 45-degree miter on the leading end of the strip. Adjust the rip fence setting so that placing the tip of the miter against the set-up block will yield a slightly oversize triangular key **(A)**. Then make the cut, holding the thin key material down with a sturdier stick of wood **(B)**. To make the next key, simply flip the spline strip over and repeat the process. Before gluing the keys in place, check the fit of each in its slot. A key should press in with some resistance, but without a fight **(C)**.

After installing the triangular keys, let the glue cure thoroughly. Then trim away most of the projection with a chisel, paring inward to prevent splitting the grain at the corner **(D)**. Flush up the remainder with a few strokes from a razor-sharp block plane.

[TIP] Keys of a contrasting wood can serve as an attractive design element in many projects.

Pare and plane
inward from
corner.

Key grain runs
perpendicular
to joint line.

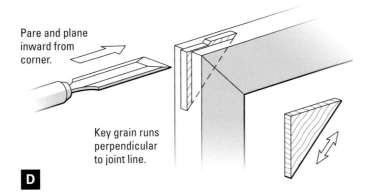

D

Making Finger Joints

Mount your dado head on the saw, stacking it to match the desired finger width, then set up your saw with your finger joint jig. Adjust the jig's fence so that the indexing pin sits exactly one finger's distance away from the blade. The best approach here is to use a spacer that was made from the pin stock **(A)**. Adjust the height of the blade to be slightly less than the thickness of your stock.

➤ See "Finger Joint Jig" on p. 180.

Check the setup by making a test joint in scrap stock that matches the thickness of your actual workpiece material. Butt the stock up against the pin, and saw the first slot **(B)**. Next, slip the slot over the indexing pin and cut the second slot **(C)**. Proceed all the way across the workpiece in this fashion until all the slots are cut.

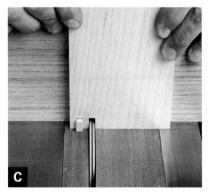
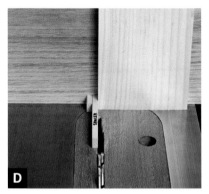

To cut the slots on the mating piece, place the spacer against the pin, and butt the workpiece against the it **(D)**. This time, the first cut will be a notch instead of a slot **(E)**. Push the notch up against the pin to cut the subsequent slot **(F)**. Again, continue in this fashion all the way across the workpiece.

Put the two test pieces together **(G)**. A perfect fit will require just a bit of hand pressure to seat the joint. If it's too tight to push together, adjust the jig for slightly narrower fingers by adjusting the pin closer to the blade. If the joint is too sloppy, increase the finger width by adjusting the pin farther from the blade. Be judicious. Small adjustments make a big difference. When you have a perfect fit, cut your actual workpieces.

A

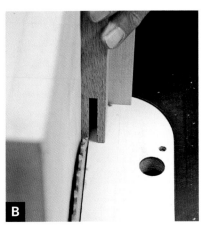

B

C

D

E

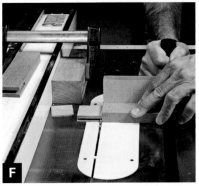

F

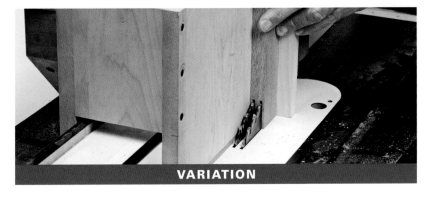

VARIATION

Bridle Joint

Set up a dado head for the desired mortise width. Set the height of the cutter to match the width of your stock. Use the rip fence to position your tenoning jig so the cut will be centered on the stock. Hold the workpieces in the jig to cut the mortise **(A)**. Make sure to use a backer to prevent exit tearout on the backside of the mortise.

[TIP] Keep the same face (I usually use the "show" face) of each piece against the jig to ensure consistent joint thickness, regardless of inconsistent stock thickness.

After cutting all your mortises, install a standard blade and set its height to match the mortise depth. With a mortised piece on the jig, set up to cut the first tenon cheek by aligning the blade with the edge of the mortise **(B)**. Then lock your rip fence in place and saw the first tenon cheek, holding the workpiece firmly against the jig **(C)**. After passing the blade, remove the piece from the jig. Don't drag it backward over the blade. Reset the fence in the same manner, and cut the second cheek **(D)**. Be sure to keep the same face of the material against the jig for both cuts.

To prepare for the shoulder cuts, adjust the blade height and place a set-up block against the rip fence. Align the outer face of the teeth with the edge of the mortised piece **(E)**. Lock the fence in place at this location. Using a miter gauge, register the end of the tenon against the set-up block, then cut the shoulders **(F)**. If your tenon isn't perfectly centered, you may need to cut all the shoulders on one side of the workpieces first, then reset the height for the opposite shoulders.

[VARIATION] The cheeks of a two-shouldered tenon like this could be cut at once by using spacers (blade stabilizers and thin shims will work) between two standard blades. A zero-clearance throat plate is a must for this operation.

Four-Shoulder Tenon with Dado Head

Although a four-shoulder tenon can be cut with a tenoning jig, I often find it quicker to cut the joint on the flat using a dado head. This method is particularly easier if the tenon is centered, which it usually is. Put your dado head on the saw—its exact width isn't important. Then set up the shoulder cut.

Holding the workpiece against the miter gauge, align the cutline with the blade and lock the rip fence against the end of the stock **(A)**. Next, adjust the blade height, which establishes the tenon thickness. Set the height just a bit shy of the layout line, and make a cut at the end of the piece **(B)**. Flip the piece over, and do the same on the other side **(C)**.

Test the fit in your mortise. It will probably be a bit too fat, so raise the cutter just a tad, and repeat the cutting process on both sides until the tenon pushes into its mortise **(D)**. If it's a little too tight, good. Let it be for the moment. Finish cutting both sides up to the shoulder **(E)**. Raise the cutter as necessary and cut the narrow shoulders, feeding the stock on edge against the miter gauge **(F)**.

Slight inconsistencies in stock thickness (which are to be expected) will lead to tenons of similarly differing thicknesses. That's why it's sensible to leave the tenons a tad fat initially. Finish up by trimming each joint to a perfect fit in its mortise using a shoulder plane **(G)** or 150-grit sandpaper wrapped around a hardwood block.

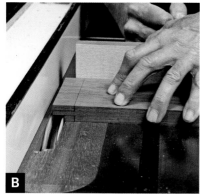

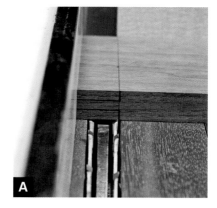

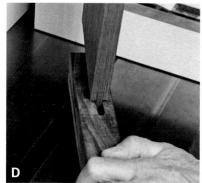

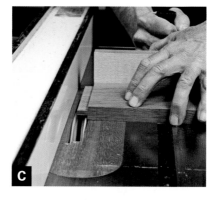

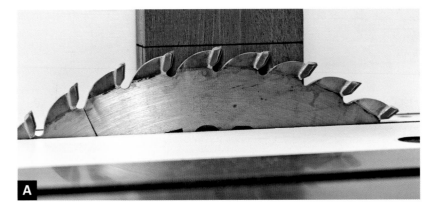

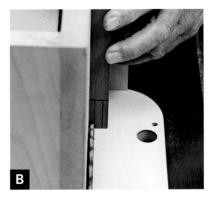

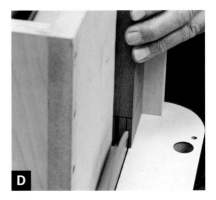

Four-Shoulder Tenon with Tenoning Jig

Begin by setting the blade height to your shoulder layout line **(A)**. Hold your workpiece against a tenoning jig and align the blade with the cheek layout line **(B)**. Then saw the first cheek on all of the pieces **(C)**. Keeping the same face against the jig, adjust the rip fence, and make the second cheek cuts **(D)**. Rotate the stock 90 degrees on the jig, reset the rip fence, and saw the narrow cheeks on the edge of the stock **(E)**.

Set up to cut the shoulders, referencing the end of the tenon against a set-up block clamped to your rip fence. The block prevents the freed offcut from jamming between the blade and the fence and kicking back. Extend the auxiliary miter gauge fence all the way to the blade so it serves as a backer to prevent exit tearout. Adjust the blade height, and saw the wide shoulders **(F)**. Stand the stock on edge, and adjust the blade height if necessary to cut the narrow shoulders to full depth **(G)**.

As you can see, this approach involves several more steps than cutting a four-shoulder tenon with a dado head. However, if you always reference the same face (inner or outer) against the tenoning jig, your tenons should all end up very nearly the same thickness, regardless of any inconsistencies in stock thickness.

Dressing and Shaping Operations

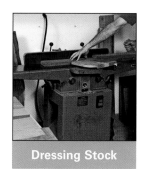

Dressing Stock

➤ Dressing Roughsawn Stock (p. 209)

Cutting Shapes

➤ Simple Tapering Jig (p. 211)

➤ Adjustable Tapering Jig (p. 212)

➤ Pattern Sawing (p. 213)

Making Bends

➤ Kerf Bending (p. 214)

Making Moldings

➤ Making a Molding (p. 215)

Cutting Coves

➤ Coving (p. 216)

B Y NOW, YOU'VE PROBABLY FIGURED out that the tablesaw does an excellent job of cutting pieces to size, squaring up ends, and creating accurate joints. What I want to share with you now are some of the saw's capabilities in terms of *shaping* wood—creating pieces that aren't necessarily rectilinear. (Although, as you'll see, the tablesaw plays a critical role in making pieces of wood rectangular to begin with.)

In this section, we dip into the ways a tablesaw can be put to use shaping wood, starting with its role in getting rough stock ready to work with. From there, I discuss tapering and cutting odd-shaped pieces. Then we take a look at the role a tablesaw can play in creating bent-wood pieces through a technique known as kerf bending. Finally, I show you two ways in which you can turn your tablesaw into a shaper. One requires a molding head and assorted cutters to cut decorative profiles, and the other uses a standard blade to make wide cove cuts.

Dressing Stock

The tablesaw is an essential tool for *dressing* stock—making it straight, square, and flat. Warped or out-of-square workpieces invite hair pulling when building cabinets and

In addition to milling a straight edge on a board, a jointer will flatten a face to prepare the board for thickness planing.

furniture, causing assemblies to rack, twist, and act generally uncooperative.

In addition to a tablesaw, you'll also want a jointer and a planer for dressing stock. Jointers flatten and straighten workpieces, while planers mill them to consistent thickness. If you don't have a jointer and planer, you can do the flattening and thicknessing with handplanes; but it's slow, sweaty work and frankly not very enjoyable after a while. The tablesaw, jointer, and planer working in unison will take care of this drudgery quickly and accurately, letting you get on with the fun of cutting joints and assembling your project.

There's a specific sequence for dressing stock to yield the desired results. In a nutshell, it goes like this:

1. Flatten one face on the jointer.
2. Plane the piece to consistent thickness.
3. Joint one edge straight.
4. Rip to width.
5. Crosscut to length.

I describe the process in step-by-step fashion later in this section. If it seems just a bit complicated at first, don't worry. It will become second nature after a while. But get in the practice, because it's a crucial process for successful woodworking.

▶ See "Dressing Roughsawn Stock" on p. 209

Tapering

Tapering is a fairly common shaping operation, often performed when making table legs. Tapering requires a jig to hold the workpiece at an angle while feeding it forward through the blade. Commercial tapering jigs made of square aluminum tubing are commonly available for about $20. Unfortunately, these don't hold their adjustments very well or grip the stock securely to the jig. This can make for a dicey cutting operation that invites kickback, particularly if you're not using a splitter. Better jigs are available for more money but it's not hard to make your own.

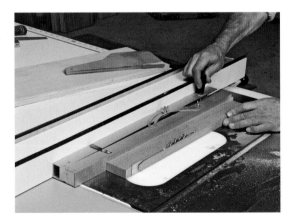

This commonly available aluminum tapering jig doesn't provide a way to secure the stock sideways to the jig, making for a somewhat dicey cutting operation.

This Woodhaven Taper Master jig rides in a miter gauge slot. It is hefty, versatile, and well designed for all sorts of tapering jobs.

You can notch a plywood panel to hold the workpiece at the proper angle for tapering a piece of a specific size and shape.

▶ WORKING WITH ROUGHSAWN STOCK

As you have probably noticed, much of the surfaced lumber available at home supply stores or lumberyards is warped—sometimes badly. That's because after surfacing, it is put into the lumber racks where it continues to move in reaction to ambient temperature and humidity. Unfortunately, if you need to dress this stuff straight, flat, and square, you often end up milling away more thickness than you can afford.

That's why most serious cabinetmakers and furniture builders buy roughsawn stock to build their projects. Available at many dedicated lumber suppliers and mills, roughsawn stock has been seasoned and stored in its unplaned state, leaving you to do the dressing yourself, creating flat, square pieces in the process. The thickness of roughsawn lumber is designated by quarters of an inch (4/4, 5/4, 6/4, 8/4, and so on.) Figure on wasting about ¼ in. of thickness in the milling process. For example, if you want to end up with ¾-in.-thick stock, buy 4/4 lumber.

You can easily make a single-purpose tapering jig by notching a piece of plywood, as shown later in this section. A carefully cut notch will hold the workpiece snugly enough for safe cutting, although it's not as good as clamping the workpiece to a jig. This approach works only for a particular size and shape, but such jigs are cheap and easy to make as needed.

▶ See "Simple Tapering Jig" on p. 211.

This tapering jig, which rides against the fence, includes toggle clamps and a stop block for securing the workpiece during the cut.

A better, safer jig can be made nearly as quickly but requires a couple of toggle clamps (available from many woodworking supply houses.) You'll also need a sled panel, a fence, and a stop block. The fence on this jig is screwed to the sled at the angle necessary to create your desired taper. The jig can be quickly modified to accommodate a variety of tapers.

Another purpose for tapering is making wedges for joints, like wedged tenons, and general shimming purposes. You can make quick work of this by building a simple hinged jig that screws to your saw's stock miter gauge.

Craig Bentzley's wedge-making jig consists of two pieces of plywood hinged together and screwed to a miter gauge. A chest lid stay secures the desired angle.

Shaping with a Sled

To cut oddly shaped pieces (pentagons, trapezoids, and the like) load them on to a crosscut sled in such a way that your cutline is aligned with the kerf in the sled. The easiest approach is simply to nail through scrap sections of the workpiece into the sled panel in such a way that the keeper piece is still secured at the end of the cut. Leave the nail heads proud for easy removal afterward. If you can't nail through the keeper piece, support it with temporary fences nailed to the sled. Hold the piece firmly down and against the fences when making the cut. This is a great way to cut the occasional odd-shaped piece. If you have number of identical odd-shaped pieces to cut, consider pattern sawing instead.

Oddly shaped pieces like this irregular pentagon can be sawn by tacking the workpiece blank directly to the panel of a crosscut sled.

Rather than tacking through the workpiece, you can hold it against fences that you've temporarily tacked to the sled panel.

Sawing Multiples

Pattern sawing allows you to quickly make identical multiples of a shape by running the edge of a pattern along a guide board clamped to the fence. The pattern

With pattern sawing, the sawblade aligns with the edge of a guide board clamped to the fence. Feeding the pattern along the guide board cuts the attached workpiece to the same shape.

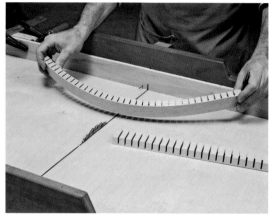

By cutting a series of deep, closely spaced saw kerfs in the back side of a workpiece you can bend it to a desired shape.

is attached to the workpiece; and because the edge of the teeth align with the edge of the guide board, the blade trims the workpiece to the exact shape of the pattern.

The guide board needs to be wide enough to create a reservoir for the offcuts between the blade and the fence. It also needs to be long enough to support the edge of the pattern before and after the cut. If the waste section is almost wide enough to reach the fence, it's best to remove the bulk of the waste first with a bandsaw or jigsaw to prevent large offcuts from wedging between the blade and the fence. The pattern should be at least $1/2$ in. thick. That way, even if an errant adjustment causes the blade to cut a bit into the pattern, enough edge will remain for solid bearing against the guide.

▶ See "Pattern Sawing" on p. 213.

Kerfing for Bending

One way to bend wood is to cut a series of deep, closely spaced saw kerfs in the backside of the piece. By leaving a thin layer of uncut wood on the face side, the piece is allowed to bend at the kerfed areas. Kerf bending creates a slightly faceted surface on the show side, so the result won't be as attractive as steam-bent or strip-laminated work. That said, it does have useful applications when aesthetics aren't a primary concern.

The best way to calculate the proper kerf spacing and depth is to make a test piece of the same size and species of your project piece. The tighter the curve, the closer the kerfs need to be. Start by spacing the kerfs about 1 in. apart and adjust from there. As for depth, you'll typically want to leave no more than about $1/8$ in. of uncut thickness and maybe as little as $1/16$ in. Play with it.

To hold its desired curve, the piece will have to be fixed to a form or bracing of some sort. Another option would be to glue a thin, bendable strip to the kerfed face. Even then, the kerfs will show at the edge of the piece and may need to be covered with edging or filled with epoxy.

Using a Molding Head

A tablesaw can be used as a sort of shaper by outfitting it with a molding head. As shown

Each of these profiles was created using a single knife set in a molding head.

These moldings were created by making a series of cuts with a variety of cutters as well as saw cuts from a standard blade.

When employing only a section of a knife, you'll need an auxiliary fence with a cutout to accommodate the unused section.

in Section 3, a molding head will accept various cutter styles that can be used to create all sorts of shapes. Used on its own, a single knife set will cut a specific profile on the edge or face of a workpiece. Complex moldings can be created by making a series of cuts, each using a different set of knives.

▶ See "Molding Heads" on p. 64.

Cutting molding isn't complicated, but there are a few things to keep in mind. First of all, use featherboards or other hold-downs to ensure clean, consistent, safe cuts. Use stock that you've dressed straight, flat, and square—if it isn't consistent in thickness and width, your featherboards won't work properly. In some cases, you'll need to set up an auxiliary fence to bury the unused section of a cutter.

> ⚠ **WARNING Always bury the unused section of a knife in an auxiliary fence. Never cut with the workpiece trapped between the knife and the fence!**

Whenever possible, cut on the flat instead of feeding the stock on edge. If a particular cut requires removing a lot of stock, do it in stages to minimize the chance of kickback. When making narrow moldings, it's best to cut them on a wide board, then rip the molding strips free afterward.

It's fun to design your own custom moldings by combining various cuts. The best approach here is to make a sample cut from every knife style you own, then save a short crosscut from each. You can lay out your own designs using this profile library. (Using the cutter itself for layout purposes won't yield the proper result because it is angled in use.) Remember that you can use just a section of a profile; orient a cut vertically or horizontally; raise, lower, or tilt the cutter;

A profile library of cuts made with your knives allows easy layout of custom moldings.

and work with the fence on either side of the blade.

When making complex moldings, it's important to perform a full practice run on a section of your prepared stock. That way, you can work out the best sequence of cuts and hold-down setups. Don't forget to save a piece of the completed molding to add to your reference library.

▶ For tips on making complex moldings, see "Making a Molding" on p. 215.

Sawing Coves

Coved trim is often used as a design element on cabinets and furniture as well as for architectural trimwork. It may surprise you that you can cut coves on the tablesaw. It's a simple matter of guiding the stock at an

The symmetrical coves at right were cut using an angled fence with the blade vertical. The asymmetrical cove at left was cut with an angled fence and a tilted blade. The raised panel is a result of half-coves.

angle over a standard blade, and taking very light successive passes. The height of the sawblade determines the depth of the cove, while the angle of the fence determines the width. The more severe the angle, the wider the cove. You can even create asymmetrical coves by tilting the blade in addition to using an angled fence.

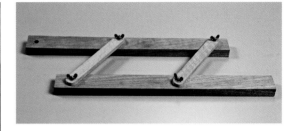

This parallelogram jig for setting up cove cuts is easy to make in any size. Just be sure that the pivot holes are equidistant from each other.

INSERT PLATES FOR MOLDING HEADS

You'll need to make insert plates for use with a molding head. If you're cutting primarily on the flat, it's okay if the opening is longer than necessary. However, for edge work, it's best to use as short a slot as possible to prevent the leading edge of the workpiece from catching on the opening.

▶ See "Making a Zero-Clearance Insert Plate" on p. 38.

You can slot the insert plate using the cutters themselves, but this can be a bit dicey because you're removing so much material. So make sure the plate is clamped down firmly, and raise the cutterhead very slowly. (Use a solid-wood plate for steel cutters, because MDF or plywood will dull them easily.) A safer approach is to cut out most of the opening with a jig-saw or scrollsaw, and then finish the job on the saw with the molding head.

You'll need to clamp an auxiliary fence to your saw table at the desired angle to guide the workpiece. The trick is establishing the correct angle, which can easily be done with a simple parallelogram jig. Fussing the setup without the jig can be frustrating, so it's worth making it.

▶ For step-by-step instructions, see "Coving" on p. 216.

Cutting this self-aligning glue joint with molding cutters requires a tight throat plate opening to prevent the leading edge of the workpiece from dropping down and snagging.

Dressing Roughsawn Stock

To prepare lumber for dressing, begin by laying out your project pieces on the boards, then cut them about ¼ in. oversize in width and a few inches oversize in length. Make sure to avoid any checks or hairline cracks, which can run far into the end of a board. To do this, first crosscut away any evident checks. Then trim off a ⅛-in. test section and flex it. If it snaps easily, it's probably cracked. Recut and repeat as necessary until the test piece holds firm **(A)**.

As you're roughing pieces out, remember to joint one edge for safe feeding against the rip fence. When everything is cut to rough size, sticker the pieces for at least a few days (a week is better) in your shop to let the wood relax and acclimate to its new shape and environment. The stickers allow air to circulate around it **(B)**.

[TIP] Before planing, you may want to relocate any critical reference marks from the face of a board to its end.

Begin the dressing at the jointer, flattening one face **(C)**. For best stability, feed the board concave side down whenever possible, and joint with the grain. Next, feed the board through the planer with the jointed face down, planing with the grain to minimize tearout **(D)**.

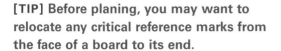

Moving back to the jointer, set the fence perfectly square to the table and joint one edge, making sure to hold the workpiece firmly against the fence **(E)**. Again, joint with the slope of the grain to minimize tearout.

Now you're ready to trim the board to finished width. For this final cut, I mount a premium-quality 40-tooth ATB blade on my saw, which

(text continues on p. 210)

F

gives me a very clean cut **(F)**. If you use a coarser blade or if you're working with wood that's prone to burning, you can set your saw's rip fence for 1/32 in. over the finished width, then trim that amount off afterward with a single pass on your jointer. (Don't take more than one pass on the jointer though, or you're likely to taper the piece.) Make the cut, being sure to orient the jointed edge against the rip fence. Keep a push stick at hand to use once the trailing end of the board rides onto the table **(G)**.

G

All that's left is to cut the piece to length, guiding it with a miter gauge or a crosscut sled. First, trim the prettier end (if there is one), taking off just enough to ensure that there is wood on both sides of the blade during the cut. This prevents sideways blade deflection, ensuring that the cut is dead square **(H)**. Finish up by marking the cutline at the other end and crosscutting the piece to final length **(I)**.

[TIP] **Whenever cutting multiples to similar lengths, use a stop on your miter gauge or sled fence to ensure that all the pieces match precisely.**

H

I

Simple Tapering Jig

Tapering can be done with a simple notched ply-wood panel that serves as a tapering jig. For this example, I show you how to taper two adjacent inside faces of a workpiece to shape a typical Shaker-style table leg. Begin by drawing your desired taper down one face of the workpiece and across its end. (This cutline begins at 5 in. down from the top of the leg.)

Make a jig board from ¾-in.-thick plywood. It should be at least 6 in. wide and a few inches longer than the leg. Place the leg on the board, aligning the cutline with the edge. Trace the pro-file of the leg onto the board **(A)**. Cut along the layout lines with a jigsaw or bandsaw **(B)**. Try to cut the ends as accurately as possible because you want the workpiece to jam snugly into the notch. (When using the jig in the future, cut the leg blanks to tightly fit the notch.)

[TIP] When tapering, cut a bit shy of your lines and clean up the sawn surface after-ward with a jointer or handplane.

Adjust your rip fence so that the edge of the template just touches the blade **(C)**, then load the workpiece into the jig. Plan your cut sequence so that an unsawn face of the leg bears against the saw table for each cut. With the workpiece seated completely in its notch, make the first cut, holding the pieces firmly against the fence **(D)**. Afterward, rotate the piece in the jig and saw the adjacent face in the same manner **(E)**.

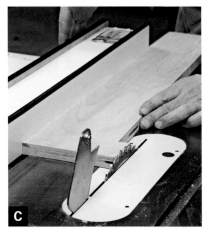

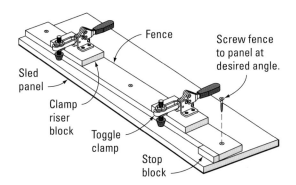

Fence

Screw fence
to panel at
desired angle.

Sled
panel

Clamp
riser
block

Toggle
clamp

Stop
block

Adjustable Tapering Jig

This adjustable tapering jig consists of a fence assembly that screws to a sled panel at whatever angle you need to make your desired taper. The fence assembly includes a stop block that's glued to the edge of the fence and two toggle clamps screwed to the top. The clamps sit on riser blocks when necessary to hold down thick stock, like this leg.

[TIP] For safe, accurate cutting, use a splitter and zero-clearance throat plate when sawing tapers with a jig.

To set up the jig, first mark the desired taper on the workpiece, then align the cutline with the edge of the sled panel, setting it in a bit so as to cut slightly shy of the line. Place the fence alongside the workpiece, butting the stop block against its end. Hold the fence in position as you screw it to the sled panel **(A)**. Plan your cut sequence so that an unsawn face will be against the jig during the cut. Clamp the workpiece to the jig, then make your first cut **(B)**. Rotate the workpiece 90 degrees in the jig, again butting it firmly against the fence stop. Use the wedge-shaped offcut as a clamp shim, and make the second cut in the same manner **(C)**.

A

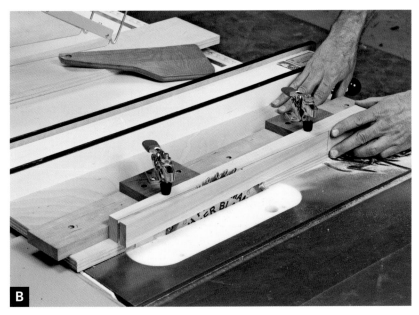

B

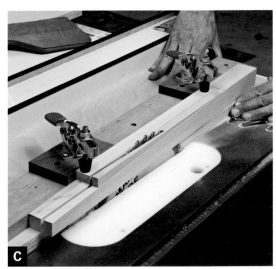

C

Pattern Sawing

Clamp your guide board to the rip fence so it rides just a bit above the height of the work-piece. I place ¼-in. shims atop the workpiece blank as set-up spacers, clamping the board to my auxiliary tall fence **(A)**. Set the blade height just above the workpiece but below the guide board **(B)**. Carefully align the left-hand edge of the teeth with the edge of the guide board. I hold a stick of wood against the guide, making sure that the teeth just barely graze it **(C)**.

Attach your pattern to the workpiece blank. One option is to drive nails or screws through the pattern into the bottom of your part if the holes will be hidden later. However, I generally use double-faced tape, smacking the two pieces hard with a mallet at the tape locations or clamping them together briefly to ensure a good bond.

Register the first edge of the pattern against the guide board. Maintain firm contact as you push the piece past the blade **(D)**. Continue around the piece in the same fashion **(E)**. Don't let the offcuts build up under the guide or they may jam between the blade and the fence. An occasional blast of compressed air from the rear of the saw will drive them out from under the guide. Alternatively, shut off the saw after every few cuts, and quickly shove the pieces out with a wide board **(F)**.

A

B

C

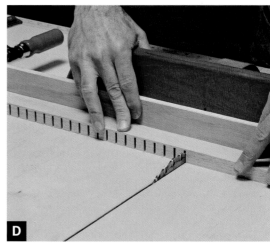

D

Kerf Bending

The technique for cutting evenly spaced kerfs for bending is similar to that for cutting finger-joint slots. As with finger jointing, a pin in an auxiliary fence serves to register each saw cut at the same distance as the previous cut. Attach the fence to your miter gauge or crosscut sled and use a finish nail as the pin. The fence should support the workpiece to both the left and the right of the blade.

▶ See "Making Finger Joints" on p. 197.

Begin by making test cuts in a scrap to determine the kerf spacing (typically in the ¾-in. to 1-in. range) and blade height that will yield your desired curve. Install a registration pin into your auxiliary fence. (The head of a #6 finish nail nicely matches a ⅛-in.-wide saw kerf.) Attach the fence to a crosscut sled (as shown here) or to a miter gauge, positioning it so the pin is the desired distance from the blade **(A)**. Make the first cut with the piece butted against the nail. Press the stock down firmly to make sure it is seated on the sled's panel **(B)**. Slip this first kerf over the pin, and make the second cut **(C)**. Continue in the same manner until you're done **(D)**.

Making a Molding

Here's an example of making a relatively simple molding using a molding head. Design your molding's profile by tracing sample pieces made with your chosen cutters **(A)**. Add lines for any modifying cuts to be made with additional cutters or a sawblade **(B)**. Plan your sequence of cuts, considering workpiece stability during the cut. For example, with this molding, the cove, V-bead, and flat between them are all cut first, leaving a temporary "leg" for stability during the cuts **(C)**. (If necessary, make your stock oversize in width for initial stability, then saw it to final width afterward.)

[TIP] **For clean, consistent, safe cuts when making moldings, use featherboards whenever possible.**

If you're using an auxiliary fence, mount it to your rip fence. Then position the fence for the first cut **(D)**. Set up your featherboards, and make the first cut **(E)**. Change cutters, and follow the same setup procedures to make the second cut **(F)**. To recess the section between the two previous cuts, mount a cutter that includes a flat section, such as this combination cutter **(G)**.

After making the molding cuts, switch to a regular sawblade to make the cut adjacent to the bead. Before setting up the featherboards this time, make test cuts, adjusting the fence and the blade height until the cut perfectly meets the bead. Then set up the featherboards as necessary to hold the work against the table and fence. In this case, the table featherboard is clamped atop riser blocks so it can apply pressure against the center of the molding. Have at hand whatever type push stick you'll need to get past the featherboards. Then make the cut **(H)**. All that's left is to saw the bevels on the back side of the molding **(I)**.

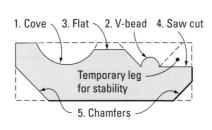
1. Cove   3. Flat   2. V-bead   4. Saw cut
Temporary leg for stability
5. Chamfers

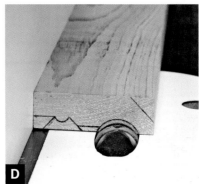

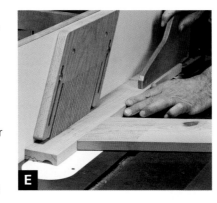

A

B

C

D

E

VARIATION

Coving

Mark the width and depth of your desired cove onto the end of your dressed stock, then set the height of the blade to match the cove depth. Set the inside edges of the parallelogram jig to the width of the cove, then lock the jig tightly at that spacing **(A)**. Place the jig over the blade, and rotate it clockwise until the front and rear teeth just graze the bars at table level. Mark a line on the table along the inner edge of the right-hand bar at each end **(B)**. Locate your fence to the right of these marks at a distance equal to the width of the cove's flat shoulder, and clamp the fence in place **(C)**. It's possible to cut the cove using just this single fence, but it's safer to set up a twin fence using the workpiece as a spacer **(D)**.

Lower the blade so it projects only about $\frac{1}{16}$ in. above the table. Feed the workpiece slowly over the blade, holding it down firmly against the table. Then take successive passes in the same manner, raising the blade about $\frac{1}{16}$ in. each time **(E)**. When you approach your final shape, make the last cut or two very light. Feed very slowly but consistently to produce as clean a surface as possible.

Expect to do some smoothing of the finely toothed surface. A curved scraper works well for the job, or you can use a custom-shaped sanding block made from stiff packing foam.

[VARIATION] A half-cove can be cut in basically the same manner, except that the fence straddles the blade. Simply clamp the fence in the desired location, and raise the spinning blade up into it as you make your successive cuts.
